LOOKING-GLASS

EUROPE
IN THE
LOOKING-
GLASS

ROBERT BYRON

HESPERUS

4

Coventry City Council	
CEN*	
3 8002 01755 171 6	
Askews & Holts	Apr-2012
914.0451	£12.00

10

Published by Hesperus Press Limited
28 Mortimer Street, London, W1W 7RD
www.hesperuspress.com

This edition first published by Hesperus Press Limited, 2012
Foreword © Jan Morris, 2012
Designed and typeset by Madeline Meckiffe
Printed by CPI Group (UK) Ltd, Croydon, CR0 4YY
ISBN: 978-1-84391-357-3

CONTENTS

FOREWORD

THAT THIS BOOK IS A PERIOD PIECE is obvious from the beginning. Its subtitle, *Reflections of a Motor Drive from Grimsby to Athens*, tells us at once that we are to be taken back to the 1920s, when the English gentry went for Motor Drives across a Europe that was still decidedly foreign, and there was still something funny to a place-name like Grimsby.

It is a comic postcard start to a book as to a journey, leading to a destination that was still hallowed in the English heart and ingrained in the English culture (for as *Murray's Handbook to Greece* had observed in 1884, in those days 'any Englishman with the usual knowledge of ancient Greek will be able to read the Athenian papers with ease'). The substance of *Europe In the Looking-Glass* (*in* the looking glass, one notes, not *through* it) is unmistakably of its time.

But in a literary sense the book is significantly of its period too, because it was one of the first of a revived literary genre – the travel book that was determinedly more than a travel book, but also a display of intellectual enterprise and distinction, a work of art and not least a worldly entertainment. In earlier times many people had written such works in English. Laurence Sterne had toyed famously with the form in *A Sentimental Journey* and Dickens had portrayed America in a related frame of mind. Mark Twain had light-heartedly toured the world; Robert Louis Stevenson had wandered the Cévennes with his donkey; and Alexander Kinglake had provided a classic model with his *Eothen*, published in 1863, describing a journey through the nearer east in a cheerfully graceful form that feels almost contemporary to this day.

But the turn of the nineteenth century was the age of Empire, of terrific adventures in exotic parts, and of war. The allures of exploration and the seductions of imperialism made for less pleasurable travel writing, and the narratives of men like Burton, Stanley and Henry Baker, set in flamboyant places and spiced with danger, their bindings gold-embossed with lions and savages, were the non-fiction best-sellers of the age. It was only in the 1920s and 1930s, when the Great War had been fought and Empire was losing its assurances, that the Kinglake tradition was revived, and Robert Byron chose his métier.

Europe in the Looking-Glass was his first book, written in 1926. He was twenty-one, fresh from Eton and Oxford and happily conscious of his remote relationship with Byron the poet. He was a clever, rather idiosyncratic, highly educated young English gentleman, and like Murray's Briton of an earlier generation, he was steeped in the mystique of classical Greece. He had escaped the miseries of the First World War, he was a child of the automobile age, and it was natural enough that his first foray into literature should be a Motor Drive to Athens, in the company of two similarly high-spirited English friends.

By the standards of his class and time he was conventionally immature, having been sent down from Oxford for misdemeanours, and he and his companions roister their way through this narrative like characters from the young Evelyn Waugh, whose contemporaries they were. For a start they did what such young men did then – they gave their car, a rather grand Sunbeam tourer, an affectionate name, Diana, rather as Stevenson had called his donkey Modestine. They behaved, too, as footloose young men of means did behave, revelling in chance encounters and comic episodes, and Byron indulged himself in a manner presently to became common among English travel writers – a kind of *faux*-incompetence and effeteness, self-portrayal verging upon caricature. Diana the car is constantly breaking down or running out of petrol, and the three young Englishmen present themselves as most decidedly not mechanically-minded.

Byron was clearly rather pleased with himself, and in this very first work of self-expression he indulges in grand judgements on art, politics and people that will sound to many readers, nearly a century on, insufferably pretentious. Ravenna, he magisterially informs us after a week or two on the Continent, is more overwhelming than anywhere else in Europe. The phenomenon of Rothenburg's conservation is without parallel in Europe. The art of the Risorgimento awaits recognition as 'one of the most meritorious intellectual phenomena of the nineteenth century'. Palladio's sense of proportion was 'unfailing'. 'There can seldom have lived a good artist with such a capacity for bad work as Bernini.'

But wait: these were the excesses of a twenty-one-year-old. As one progresses through the pages of this book, one begins to realise that they contain the early elements of a far more remarkable mind. For one thing, for all his know-all judgements the young Byron already demonstrates remarkable insights into the history and meaning of art; in this volume they are expressed most vividly in his responses to Greek classicism, later they were to be superseded by a profound admiration for the then neglected art and architecture of Byzantium. Then again, if there are some overwrought passages of prose in *Europe in the Looking-Glass*, there are also descriptions and evocations of striking beauty, to stop one suddenly in one's patronising tracks. And above all, perhaps, there is a truly mellow sense of humour, usually generous, often cynical or irreverent, occasionally waspish, which impregnates the whole work and remains more or less ageless.

The comedy is often incidental, as it were, to the theme of the moment, and generally lies in detail, and in a virtuoso choice of words. We glimpse, for instance, fisherwomen of Naples 'munching lethargically at their indescribable foods'. At a fountain at the Villa Lante at Viterbo we notice ornamental lions 'expectorating' their water towards 'recumbent' Tritons

below. And for the young Byron the character of the celebrated
Greek national costume, the fustanella, is best exhibited by
'the dirt and squalor of the old men who passed by, their short
tunic skirts frilling out above their knees, and their whole legs
swathed in bulky white wrappings tied here and there like
parcels of washing…'

But in and around the *joie de vivre* of it all, anyone can see
that there is a remarkable sensibility germinating here. In long
passages of serious description and analysis a fine intellect
is at work too. For example Byron devotes several pages to
the cathedral at Esztergom, in Hungary, which he had visited
the year before when he was hardly more than a youth. It
is a detailed, careful and perceptive technical analysis. Only
once does he lapse into his adolescent dogmatism (when
he cannot help remarking that the cathedral's high altar,
'though inoffensive, embodies the worst characteristics of
the Guercino tradition…') For the rest, having read this
undergraduate assessment few readers will be tempted to
doubt its magisterial conclusion that 'the church of Esztergom
stands alone as the finest single edifice of early nineteenth-
century architecture in existence'.

And we shall be right, for in *Europe in the Looking-Glass* we
are discovering the seed of great writing. After its title page an
author's statement declares that the book makes no pretensions
to literary merit – 'it is offered to the public in the sole hope that
the public will buy it'. In fact, a few pages later, Byron says he
hopes it will further 'the new sense of European consciousness',
and this was certainly a truer intention. For it was a first book,
very much a young man's book, and before long Robert Byron
was to mature into a writer of high learning, skill and lasting
influence, and to be the great master of that particular genre
of travel writing with which he first experimented in 1926. He
travelled constantly all his life, and became a great authority on
matters Byzantine, until six books later, in 1936, he wrote his
masterpiece *The Road to Oxiana*, which established his place
once and for all in the English literary canon.

With *Europe in the Looking-Glass* Byron was pioneering a new kind of travel writing. With *The Road to Oxiana* one can almost say that he invented another, so startlingly original was its form – a kind of artificial diary and memorandum, put together collage-like in afterthought, and declared by scholars to have had the same sort of effect upon travel writing that Eliot and Joyce had upon fiction. Certainly, by way of *Oxiana* we can the trace the influence of Robert Byron upon countless later practitioners, from Patrick Leigh-Fermor to Eric Newby to Rory Maclean (who also travelled with a car – not a Sunbeam, but a Trabant).

And many more of us, too, may feel that we have been liberated by Byron's example from the curse of the travelogue – the stigma that used to imply that travel-writing could not qualify as true literature. Alas, few of us now alive have been able to thank him. Robert Byron died in 1941, aged thirty-five, when a German U-boat torpedoed the ship in which was sailing on a BBC commission to Egypt. His body was never recovered.

– Jan Morris, 2012

PART ONE

CHAPTER I

A POLICEMAN, pacing sedately along the left side of Upper Brook Street at half-past ten on the sultry night of Friday, the 1st of August, 1925, was surprised to find stretched lengthways upon the pavement three recumbent figures, studying a map by the dim green light of a street lamp above them. Drawn up by the kerb stood a massive touring car, the back of which was entirely occupied with a mountainous pile of trunks and suitcases. The policeman, after a minute's hesitation, unbent so far as to take a glance at the map himself; and, if his eyesight was good, he may remember to this day the shadowy outline of East Anglia that spread itself beneath him, bounded on the west by the Great North Road.

'Out through Finchley,' murmured a voice, 'then past Hatfield to Peterborough, leaving Cambridge on the right.'

This was settled. The map was folded. And the three figures, David Henniker, Simon O'Neill and myself, rose to their feet and moved towards the car. With a last glance, the policeman continued on his way, stolidly scrutinizing the unending succession of area railings that lined the remainder of the street.

The preliminaries of the tour had been rather erratic. One weekend, at the beginning of May, David had arrived in Oxford and asked me to dine with him. We had had a peculiar dish of sole covered with burnt custard and muscatels. During this he suggested that I should join him and Geoffrey Pratt on 'a trip to the Balkans'. The prospect seemed delightful. We began to outline the route, but found it impossible without the aid of an atlas. Then David motored home to bed.

A few days later Wembley opened her gates a second time to a patriotic public. The first person to be seen on arrival in the Amusement Park was Simon, sitting bolt upright on the Giant Racer, in a bowler hat and gloves. He was nervously sharing a compartment with a small boy in a vermilion cap, and was immediately whisked out of sight as we arrived at the pay-box. For the past year he had been on a visit to the Galapagos Islands as part of a scientific expedition, and since his return we had not until this moment seen him – nor he Wembley.

After he had alighted and suffered the effusive greetings consequent on so long an absence, we asked him what he was doing. He said he did not know. I suggested that he should come with David to the Balkans. It would mean another car. He replied that he thought that that could be managed. At that moment the police, who were on the track of a couple of missing iron chairs, appeared round the corner. We disappeared into Hong Kong, and thence entered Trinidad by a back way, where we drank Planter's Punches. Eventually we parted in Shaftesbury Avenue.

At the beginning of July the prospective members of the party spent Friday to Monday at Highworth, David's home. It was arranged that I should go with Simon in one car, while David and Geoffrey Pratt should share the other. But three or four days afterwards Simon discovered that, for various reasons, he was unable to provide a car after all. I, therefore, realizing that all along the idea had been too good to be true, dropped out and decided to go to Ireland instead.

However, on Tuesday, the 28th of July, a wire arrived from David asking if I could leave for the Balkans on Saturday. Geoffrey Pratt, it appeared, had failed at the last minute, as his firm would only give him a fortnight's holiday. It was to be David, Simon and myself.

The next day I spent between the Passport Office and Cook's in Ludgate Circus; and the day after hurried home to pack, having a quarrel in the train with a woman in a white feather boa, who proved to be the sister of the local parson. On Friday

I returned to London; and was poised on an island at the bottom of the Haymarket, when David emerged unexpectedly from between two 'buses and said that we were starting that night. The rest of the evening passed in a fever of excitement. At ten-fifteen, accompanied by Simon, he drew up at the front door. The tour had begun.

In appearance, the party, as a whole, was not undistinguished. The car, a large touring Sunbeam, was painted a dark, nearly black, blue-grey. She was named Diana. Her lines were impressive and her bonnet long, sloping scarcely at all from the level of the tops of the doors. The tank at the back hung low, and the clearance all round was small, so that the back light and exhaust did not survive the third day's journey. On either side, resting on the front wings, were mounted two wire-spoked spare wheels to each of which was roped a spare outer cover.

The back was entirely filled with luggage. At the bottom, invisible to the policeman and undiscovered by successive customs officials, were a 30-gallon tank of petrol, a cylinder of oil, four spare springs, fifteen inner tubes in yellow cardboard boxes that all came to pieces within twenty-four hours, and an ever-increasing rubble of sticks, hats, books, magazines and stray tools. On top, resting on the seat without its cushion, stood the heavy luggage: a huge yellow cabin-trunk belonging to Simon, that protruded at least two feet above the hood; a very large brown one, the property of David; and a moderate black box of mine. In front were the lighter pieces: two suitcases, heavily fitted with coming-of-age bottles, in canvas overalls; and a very worn Gladstone bag capable of unlimited expansion. Finally, in front in a row, sat the three human units of the expedition.

As the interest, if any, of the following account must depend largely on the angles adopted towards places already familiar and adventures already commonplace, some description of the antecedents of the party may not be altogether superfluous. All three had been educated at the same school and at the same university. At the former, frequently described as 'one of our leading public schools', David had preceded Simon and myself; and even we were not contemporary. I retain a vision of him as an older boy, out beagling, running persistently and seriously across ploughed fields, with a rather prominent nose held well up in the air and light greenish blue eyes downcast.

'That,' said my informant, in whose house Simon was, 'is O'Neill. He's queer – he says he's a communist. He's very clever. Yes, I like him.'

It was 1921. 'Communist' in those days was but another word for Bolshevik, and at the time the streets of Moscow were running blood. It seemed strange, even as a pose.

The following Easter Simon left. I never knew him except by sight.

David had been taken away before the end of the war. His family had gone to Canada and he, as he was supposed to have bronchial trouble, had accompanied them. He attended a Canadian school and also MacGill University. Then he came home to Oxford. Simon and I arrived there a year later, he having spent most of 1922 at Tours, while I had remained at school.

Simon's communism is the misdirected outcome of sympathy for those less fortunate than himself. During our trip he talked vaguely of the nationalization of the banks. Otherwise he was considered at Oxford a brilliant historian. He is fond of obscure details, and paradoxes culled, from Chesterton and Belloc, which upset the views of every single authority on any given subject. His knowledge of out-of-the-way facts, such as the date of the death of the last woman who spoke Cornish, or the dimensions of the Albanian fustanella, is astonishing, though uncoordinated. He is extremely well read.

Unfortunately, his relations with his college authorities did not run smoothly. Regardless of his degree, he forsook the pleasures of university life and started to write a history of church persecution under Cromwell. Then he joined the scientific expedition. This, for some reason, elected to go in a sailing ship, and spent most of its time waiting for funds at Panama, to the complete demoralization of all on board. The town was full of American officials and their wives. Eventually they did succeed in reaching the Galapagos Islands; and were finally faced with complete starvation. By that time, however, Simon had left them.

In appearance Simon is upright and neat. He affects a pearl pin and stiff collar. Whenever possible he likes to dress for dinner. Both he and David have lost their fathers.

David is of a different type. A kind of supernatural vigour is his outstanding characteristic. He is lazy, partly because this exhausts him. But whatever he does becomes of itself remarkable.

He is slim, and possesses and wears an enormous wardrobe of fashionable, though sombre, clothes. Whereas Simon is shy and does not converse fluently with strangers, David is totally devoid of even a decent sense of embarrassment and can make inexhaustible conversation to any living creature that understands a single word of French, German or English. He also has a·knowledge of history, but his chief interests are decoration and architecture. In the latter he is a purist. To both him and Simon, Sentiment and Romance, far from palliating the defects of a building or the unauthenticity of a legend, are not only meaningless, but repellent. It was on this common ground that they differed most fundamentally from myself.

As mentioned above, Simon's knowledge of the Universe was confined to Panama, some desert islands and Tours. I had, in the spring of 1923, spent five weeks in Italy under ideal circumstances, and could claim some knowledge of that country and her monuments. I had also visited parts of Central Europe. But of the three, it was only David who possessed more than a superficial familiarity with Europe, her countries and their inhabitants. He knew France. He had experienced revolutions in Germany after the war. And in 1924 he had motored to the Russian frontier, spent six weeks in Poland, and then taken Prague, Vienna and Rome in his stride home.

This had been a most remarkable tour, which only his initiative could have carried through. It is his outstanding ambition, in fact, to make the acquaintance of the whole earth and the races with which it is peopled.

To attain a sense of the relative proportions of the various entities of which the modern world is composed, it is essential clearly to define the position occupied by the civilization of the United States. This is only possible by comparison with Europe. But Europe, taken as a whole, is such an unknown quantity to most of her inhabitants, nurtured in the disastrous tradition of the armed and insular state, that they are unable to gauge the contrast between their own corporate civilization, the laborious construction of two thousand years, and the retrograde industrialism sprung up in a night on the other side of the Atlantic. Admittedly it is not to be expected that the doings of three young men, interpreted through the pen of one of them, can prove of any serious value. But if, in providing to a certain degree, however lopsided, a picture of the continent of which England forms a part, these doings will in any way further the new sense of 'European Consciousness' that is gradually coming into being, perhaps the reader will forgive the inchoate agglomeration of trivial fact and irrelevant opinion that comprises the remainder of this book.

CHAPTER II

IT WAS WITH DIFFICULTY that we discovered the whereabouts of Finchley. The way out of London seemed to lie somewhere in the direction of the Wallace Collection and straight on. David was more or less familiar with the road, having once driven to Northallerton and back in the day. He had wished to see some panelling. On the way up he had offered a lift to a tramp, who said that he was making for York. When they reached York, the tramp expressed a wish to come on to Durham. Then, after going with David to admire the panelling, he thought that, after all, he would prefer to return to York. He eventually came the whole way back to London. It is a curious phenomenon, this passion that the unemployed display for motoring. They will willingly retrace a month's hard walking for the sake of a day's drive. Perhaps it enables them to forget their troubles.

Once through Finchley, the tramlines seemed as though they would never end. They stretched for miles into country, where there was not a house in sight. After the gates of Hatfield it became so cold that we stopped to put on overcoats. Then I fell asleep, to be wakened some time later by David's backing on to the main road, having shot up the turning to Cambridge by mistake.

At one o'clock we reached the outskirts of Peterborough. Clumps of giant factory chimneys, silhouetted against the glow of furnaces, rose from the surrounding fields. The town was deserted but for one inarticulate policeman, who seemed unable to comprehend our very natural desire for a hotel. We, at length, discovered the Angel; but an angry landlord in grey and yellow flannel pyjamas informed us that it was full. So was the Station Hotel. The Grand, however, though not possessing a garage, was able to offer us three separate rooms, each of which was furnished with a Bible stamped with the words 'The Commercial Travellers' Bible Association'. Thus hallowed, we retired to sleep, leaving Diana, containing everything we possessed, in the street.

The view next morning disclosed nothing but a waste of ruined brick, slightly charred, with the factory chimneys in the distance. In order to embark the car before the dockers stopped work, it was essential to be at Grimsby by eleven o'clock. Simon showed admirable firmness in helping David out of bed at half past seven. A bath did not offer itself. We left about nine, and as it became more and more apparent that we could not cover eighty miles in two hours we remembered that the next day was Sunday, and the day after that Bank Holiday, and pictured ourselves enjoying a healthy weekend romping about on the sands of the Humber. Diana had not been 'run in', and could not exceed a speed of forty miles an hour.

After leaving the fen country, we reached the wold country, reminiscent of perhaps the most picturesque of all our laureates. It was hard to think that we must miss that Gothic fireplace, standing but half-a-dozen miles from the main road, which young Alfred and his father had built with their own hands. But it was twelve o'clock before we reached the docks at Grimsby. These appeared to be completely empty. We drove endlessly in and out of bridges, cranes and railway lines, until we eventually found the ship unaided.

A corpulent man in a uniform then emerged from a shed. He said that there would be no difficulty, no difficulty whatever. David's grandfather, it appeared, owned most of the line. No sooner was his name invoked than we were treated with embarrassing deference. After emptying Diana of her petrol, we picked our way back to the Royal Hotel to lunch, where the waitress, on being asked whether the sole was fresh, drew herself up and replied that she was not in the fish trade.

We returned to find the car safely on board, roped to a kind of wooden tray. We were due to meet the customs man at two. He did not arrive until four. By that time the steward had gone on shore to tea, taking with him the key of the ladies' lounge in which were locked our suitcases and the papers for the car. He was, therefore, unable to fill in the preliminary paragraphs of the *Carnet,* a sort of international motor pass – as distinct from the *triptyque* – which holds good for France, Italy, Czechoslovakia, and one or two other countries. That the validity of the form depended entirely upon the declaration of the customs of the country from which the motor had originally come, this man did not mention.

Our ship, by name the *Accrington,* a small and slightly squalid boat, was obliged, owing to the vagaries of the tide, to leave the dock about five. We went off in a tender, half-an-hour later, having taken a taxi and done some shopping in the meanwhile. David, having left London in a bowler, provided himself with a high quality Panama; Simon purchased a library of Oppenheims; and I bought a postcard of a view of the docks taken from the air. In addition, we took on board the *Times,* the *Sketch,* the *Tatler, Vogue, John Bull,* the *Daily Express,* the *London Mail,* the *Methodist Times,* and the *Nation.*

Once safely aboard, it was not long before David received a visit from the Dock Superintendent, a horsey-looking man in his anecdotage, with the usual grievance against the authorities. He hoped we were comfortable. At dinner we were ushered to seats opposite him, and he and David kept up a vivacious chatter about fishing rights off the Iceland coast. About half-past eight he left. We drank a little beer to settle the stomach and went to bed at eleven. David and Simon shared the state-room. I had an ordinary cabin to myself. The state-room had brass beds, not berths.

The morning of Sunday dawned sunny, but rough. The sea was a deep blue, flecked with white. For the moment I felt rather peculiar as I clung to my brass railings or fell heavily against the iron-studded side of the ship. At nine the steward, all attention, appeared with tea and toast. This enabled us to

dress for lunch. The day passed without event. We went and
lay up in the forepart of the ship, and David made offering
to Neptune down the anchor-hole when no-one was looking.
This may have been due to the nauseous odour of the fish
manure with which the hold was filled. Fish manure, so the
steward informed us, was the most flourishing export industry
of modern times. As pleasure traffic to Germany was still
non-existent, it was the only means by which the ships were
enabled to pay their way at all. Towards evening it became
even rougher, and two odious little boys, who had formerly
stalked about the ship calling one another 'old chap', were now
conspicuous by their absence – or rather by the noises that
emerged from their cabin, which adjoined the smoking-room.

At length, land was sighted on the right. This was followed
by Heligoland on the left. Then it grew dark and we went to
bed. Gradually we passed Cuxhaven and entered the mouth of
the Elbe, and lights shone out from either shore. I must confess
to a childish excitement when arriving anywhere by ship, and
was perpetually poking my head out of the porthole at the
sound of a whistle or the flash of a signal lamp. Naturally,
therefore, just as it was becoming light, I fell asleep and did
not awaken till we were moored fast to the quay at Hamburg.

The scene was one of tremendous activity. All around
towered vast warehouses in the German manner, great expanses
of blank brick, surmounted by stretch upon stretch of shining
roofs in irregular triangles, like the settings of a modern film.
In the air was the tang of salt water and that clear, fresh smell
of towns on early summer mornings that is quite distinct
from the proverbial freshness of the country dawn. Great
long timber barges, with squat black, shingled roofs, were
hurried past by tiny little tugs. On the quay, stalwart dockers
were busy manoeuvring enormous packing-cases, rained on
them by innumerable cranes. Motor-boats, containing pilots
and harbour police, were flying in all directions. And in the
distance, red, black, and white, loomed the funnels of the great
liners, softened through a faint haze of smoke.

By eight o'clock, save for us and a swarm of German stevedores and officials, the *Accrington* was empty. German bureaucracy had risen to the occasion of Diana's arrival. Each official spoke perfect English and displayed a paternal kindness, which contrasted strongly with the disobligingness that usually distinguishes the ports of France. A benign figure in uniform, facially the image of the Kaiser, busied himself with our passports as soon as we had bathed; while a living replica of the Crown Prince, bearing his lunch in a crocodile bag, had been deputed by the RAC to attend to the car. After many unpleasant moments, and a reformation of the whole dock in order that ship and crane might meet, Diana was landed uninjured on dry land. We bade the steward goodbye, and accompanied by the Crown Prince and the Kaiser, marched on shore. The latter, radiating good-fellowship, guided us by the arm and made little jokes.

'You will now 'ave to drrive to the rright. This is no longerr England. Ha, ha, ha. He, he, he!'

We all piled on the car and motored round the corner to a customs yard. There we remained for three hours.

We were now in the midst of the warehouses. Cliffs of unrelieved brick hemmed us in on every side, till the sky was scarcely visible. Incident was forthcoming in the cruelties of the waggon-drivers, one of whom, finding his horses unable to get a huge load of barrels started, beat them so unmercifully that they fell to the ground in a sheet of flame caused by the contact of hoof and paving-stone. Naturally our British blood boiled, and in company with other drivers, we ran to the rescue. The unfortunate animals, however, seemed better able to rise to their feet unaided. At the same time, nowhere in England could one have found cart-horses so well tended or in such good condition.

Meanwhile David was arguing his way from one official to another, deeper and deeper into the warehouses, over the subject of paying a deposit on legitimate spare parts. After an interminable time, a compromise was arrived at, though even this was expensive enough. It was nearly one o'clock by the time we had driven into the more fashionable quarter, where, after filling up with petrol, we had lunch at an hotel on the front of one of the large lakes round which the town is built. The decorations were modern and ugly, consisting of Prussian blue material and brass, the latter mostly fretted by a key pattern. The food was good. At half-past two we found our way to the suburbs and set off for Berlin.

CHAPTER III

THE NORTH GERMAN PLAIN on that August afternoon wore an air of tranquil beauty, not usually connected with the popular visualization of its expressionless surface. Flat, and even in the golden light of sunset unavoidably grey, it exhibits all the agricultural features that make otherwise uninteresting country attractive. And the view offered by any slight rise in the land is infinite. The fields are small, with hedges; and, as it was harvest time, many were filled with corn-cocks that threw long shadows on the dry yellow stubble. Labourers, men and women, were working late into the evening, gleaning and carting. Here and there small pinewoods, perhaps surrounding an unpretentious country house, formed dark patches on the landscape. Everything seemed at right angles, the side roads to the main road, and the hedges and furrows to both. But once away from the main road, this regularity no longer prevailed.

The half-timbered, red-brick buildings of the villages and farmhouses were surmounted by immense moss-grown expanses·of steep-sloping roof. Even those houses and barns that were modern had preserved this style, reminiscent of many of Durer's etchings, particularly that of the Prodigal Son among the Swine, though Durer, in fact, came from the south. Each village contains a war memorial – or sometimes two, the first dating from 1870 – executed in the style of an advertisement for eugenics; and a parish church that has the appearance of having been designed by an architect who, though unable to draw, knew his way about a box of toy bricks.

The road, at first abominable, improved in the province of Brandenburg. *Pavé* and asphalt seemed to alternate, while at the side was left a 'rotten row' for carts, from one of which a fat wench threw an apple that hit Simon on the head, most part flanked on either side were rows of small trees, either chestnuts, elms that did not look like elms, or apples laden with fruit. These, by their continual dripping, had evidently destroyed any surface that the road might once have possessed. Every now and then a large stretch would be completely closed for repairs, which entailed either making circuitous detours by side roads, or removing barriers and blocks of stone in the face of protesting workmen. After one excursion into the countryside, which ended in a bog, the latter course seemed preferable, though even after the menders had left work there was always some officious cyclist to champion their violated rights.

At intervals couples of *Wandervögel*, open-necked youths with flaxen hair and khaki shirts and shorts, would wave a greeting as we passed. Some were carrying guitars. Our acquaintance with their species was destined to ripen into intimacy as we travelled further south.

Other motors were scarce. Benz, Mercedes, Austro-Daimler, and a few Italian cars, are almost the only makes to be seen in Germany. The light car is practically unknown.

After passing through Ludwigslust and Kyritz, we arrived in Spandau, an industrial suburb of Berlin, just as it was beginning to grow dark, having taken six hours to drive two hundred miles without a single stop. To David's delight, we found ourselves upon a newly-made approach to the capital, as wide and as long as the Great West Road out of London, only more effective, inasmuch as it is perfectly straight, slopes downhill, and is for the most part flanked on either side by groups of high modern buildings, grey and rather ornamented, horrible in detail, but successful as a whole. Below us the lights of the city began to twinkle. About eight o'clock we drove through the Potsdammerplatz and up to the front door of the Esplanade Hotel, the staff of which was impressed by our arrival. Large airy rooms on the first floor, looking out through French windows on a garden courtyard and containing every comfort known to science, had been reserved by telephone from Hamburg. We dressed and went down to dinner about half-past nine, to find the restaurant at its fullest. We ate caviare as large as frog spawn and blue trout that looked like Ming pottery. Afterwards we sauntered out, and, to Simon's disgust, walked a long distance in search of a café that did not exist. Berlin's amusements have been censored since the immediate postwar days. Very tired we at length returned to bed – or rather to an eiderdown buttoned on all sides to a sheet.

There was little inducement to arise next morning, with a library of detective stories at hand and a *Berliner Tagblatt* included in the tray of breakfast. However, I was down before the others, with a view to changing some money at the *Deutsche Bank*. But in spite of the most precise and categorical directions, I was unable to find it. The hotel, therefore, supplied me with a diminutive page, who marched me through the streets with that pompous, measured tread that one usually connects with bishops in the rear of processions. This called forth hoots of ridicule from other boys engaged in window-cleaning and doorstep-scrubbing. Finally I was left in the hands of an obese commissionaire, from whose chin descended a luxuriant growth of grizzled beard parted in the middle. Instead of directing me to the Letter of Credit Department, he impelled me into the middle of the road, and with the gestures of a Franciscan preacher, proceeded to declaim the glories of his bank: not only was this side of the street all *Deutsche Bank*, but also that. What beautiful buildings! and what we saw here was not all; there was more round the corner. Round the corner we went; I changed my money; and taking a short cut for foot passengers only, came out on the Unter den Linden, next door to a barber's, into which I went, as my hair needed cutting. It was with difficulty that the man could be persuaded to take enough off, so alarmed was he lest he should be thought to admire the ordinary shaven scalp of his country. An English *Weekly Graphic* showed pictures of Simon's expedition removing the stone engraved with an Inca inscription that Simon had discovered on the beach of some remote islet. Simon himself was not visible; nor did he appear to have accompanied the others in their friendly advances to the giant lizards six feet long, that had previously existed only in the illustrations to Wells' *History of the World*.

After buying a piece of soap I walked down the Unter den Linden to the broad space at the end, and entered the Kaiser Frederick Museum. Being as yet unfamiliar with their native surroundings, the naturalism of the Greek sculptures seemed to convey to me little more than photography in three dimensions. The masterpiece of the collection is a superb head of Athene by Pheidias. Only the greatest sculptors have realised that one side of the human face is seldom a symmetrical counterpart of the other. The museum was full of family parties ranging from infancy to dotage, all doing their duty by the famous works of art and reading to one another analyses of the respective merits of the statues from out of large but closely-printed handbooks. The salient feature of the building was, however, a penetrating smell, reminiscent of washing hung to dry before the kitchen stove. This drove me out. Next door was the cathedral, which I tried to enter, but, unfortunately, by the wrong door, and found myself sitting in a queue of stranded mothers seeking charity. After a few minutes' rest, I returned to the hotel on top of a 'bus. Simon and David were dressed, and we went to the Bristol Bar – where everyone in Berlin is said to drink cocktails before lunch.

'Everyone' consisted of an American in a straw hat talking business with another in a Lincoln Bennett Hamberg bound in white; an Englishman in chocolate suede shoes and a Guards' moustache, who looked as if he had been turned out of England; and a Mr Hutten, London-tailored, a friend of David's early days in Germany, who now conducts a furniture business in New York. I heard of him when I returned to England, from other sources. He told us to lunch at Pelzer's. Simon explained that the plethora of 'Bristol' Hotels in Europe was due to the restlessness of a former Lord Bristol, also a bishop, who travelled so incessantly and in such magnificence, that the very fact of his having stopped at an hotel gave it a reputation which it could only preserve by assuming his name.

We lunched at Pelzer's in a bower formed of gilded trellis-work and real vines, the back of which was decorated with scene-painters' landscapes. I ate nothing. David had a haunch

of venison stuffed with foie gras and covered. with cherries,
but was too lazy to touch it. Afterwards Simon went home to
read, while David and I scoured the city for a cinema. None
were open till six o'clock. Berlin has not sunk to the depravity
of afternoon amusements.

That evening, after dining early, we drove out to
Charlottenburg to a musical comedy called 'Anna Marie'.
The hotel had reserved us seats in the front row; but when
we arrived late there were only two instead of three. David
fell into the most extravagant rage and abused the officials, old
men in pinces-nez, with such effect that they compelled a man
to vacate his seat for one of us. Then Simon decided that it
was too hot and that he would prefer to sit in the beer garden
outside after all. So David and I went in alone, in the middle of
the act, to the very audible annoyance of the audience.

The cast consisted of five. The leading man was bald and
dressed in tennis clothes, perfected by a college tie and leather
belt. The leading lady was pretty, but her mass of fluffy yellow
hair, done over one eye, and a set smile, redolent of the Victorian
music hall stage, rather detracted from her charms. Her clothes
were 1923. The phenomenal idea of an evening scarf attached to
the dress had reached Berlin in the same breath as it had gone
out of fashion elsewhere. At the end, with a wickedly indecent
high kick, she disclosed a long pair of thick purple drawers
reaching to the knee. But the favourite was a very fat old woman
in a tight, sleeveless modern dress and bangles, her hair done
in a chignon, who burlesqued the others, flinging her plump
calves from side to side and singing in a high, raucous, and
rather pathetic voice. The tunes were delightful and composed
by the brothers Gilbert. At length the whole backcloth began to
revolve, displaying an illuminated panorama of Berlin at night,
and all five danced in front as it went round behind them. The
plot was snobbish, Anna Marie being a girl of noble birth, which
she conceals, in order to induce the bald man, the love of her
life, to marry her in a suburban back garden. The transports
of her husband's family when they discovered her origin were

touching, and even her father, in a frock coat and top hat, was reconciled. This is a favourite theme for continental comedy and light opera. We saw it repeated several times in Italy and once on a film, in which the girls at a convent school bullied the life out of one of their number, because she was the daughter of a cocoa king – '*uno cacao-re*'.

In the intervals we rejoined Simon in the garden; the band beneath the trees would repeat the tune of the act before; and it was a sight that filled the heart with pleasure to see the whole audience, mostly consisting of short, fat women in dark skirts and white blouses, swaying to and fro to the prevailing lilt, with pint mugs of yellow Pilsener beer held tightly in their right hands.

About half-past eleven we drove to the Adlon Bar to meet Mr
Hütten. He appeared in a bowler hat, with a friend. They were
to show us the Berlin underworld. This was some way away
and we went in a taxi, the driver of which was ashamed of us.
Eventually we arrived at an orange door in the slums flanked by
two box trees. Beyond it was a room that resembled the lounge
of a station hotel in the Midlands. At one table at the back, David
espied his friend, Henry Featherstonhaugh, attaché in Prague,
seated with the son of a member of the German Cabinet, and
some other more beautiful companions. The vigour of David's
recognition caused him some embarrassment. He combined
incomparable pomp of manner with extreme cynicism. His
friend, dark and sinister, purred suavely about the charm of
travel. Other people collected, and we formed a larger and larger
ring, finally returning to bed about half-past one.

The next morning, in company with a large crowd, we
gazed at Hindenburg's windows. He did not appear. After a
sleepy afternoon we dined at a Russian restaurant. This was
not one of the up-to-date, semi-smart establishments that are
so common in Paris, but a small, sordid, double room on the
ground floor, run simply for the benefit of some of the three
hundred thousand exiles in Berlin. The menu was printed in
Russian, and so were the newspapers. We ate the traditional
salad and drank kwass and vodka, the former tasting like
strong, but not dark, sweetened beer. After dinner we
proceeded to the 'Elysium', of which we became members on
the spot. Simon was good enough to consider that my having
been posted that morning in the *Times* as recipient of third-
class honours in history, warranted a bottle of champagne.
This caused a sensation. Not only did the movable units of the
band transplant themselves and their instruments to the backs
of our chairs, but the proprietor himself arrived, extremely
thirsty. He was followed by a 'friend'. The 'friend' passed
some champagne to another 'friend', who also joined the circle.
Bottles arrived automatically. We were in evening dress and
felt that we were raising the tone of Berlin.

Eventually, at closing time, the manager was so overcome that he beseeched us to return with him to his flat and 'have a drink'. This was the last thing we wanted. However, off we drove in a body through impenetrable labyrinths and rows of narrow streets, until at length, after feeling our way through a courtyard, we were ushered into three rooms and a bathroom-kitchen on the ground floor of a large tenement building. The sitting room was the home of the coloured photograph *in excelsis:* life-size men with square beards and pink faces against blue skies, alternated with their wives in high sleeves and gold lockets. Next door, in a worn copper bath, reposed a mass of dirty socks in thick, grey water; while the remainder of the washing, cuddling to itself the kitchen utensils, cried to Heaven from the top of an old trunk.

By four o'clock it was raining hard. We left, to awake next morning with a slight feeling of nausea, which decided us to leave Berlin at once.

Nevertheless, from the point of view of talking German, our evenings had been a great success.

Berlin has a pleasant atmosphere. Unlike Paris, it is far enough away from London to feel as if it were somewhere else. The Unter den Linden is magnificent. Whereas in Vienna the famous ' Rings' are entirely spoilt by the rows of plane trees that obscure them, this is wide enough to carry its double avenue. The traffic is sparse and slow. The streets are well kept and the tramlines run through the little lawns, green and well watered, that are planted in the squares, so that men are to be seen carefully cutting round them with pairs of shears. The Brandenburger Tor, surrounded by the palaces of the nobility, compares favourably with the unruined ruin at Hyde Park Corner or the flamboyance of the Arc de Triomphe. And the people are friendly – far more friendly than in France or Italy. It is this, after all, that counts most in the impression that a city gives.

CHAPTER IV

THE DISTANCE FROM BERLIN TO NUREMBERG is three hundred and twelve miles. We had intended to start at eight o'clock, but were none of us dressed until ten. The garage was situated at the other end of the town, and the car was deposited in a cellar reached by a lift. When it came to the surface, it had to be oiled, greased and filled with petrol. Also a valve needed adjusting. The heat of the sun was intense and paralysed our actions. On our way back to the hotel we passed Henry Featherstonhaugh, bouncing along in a black satin tie and Oxford trousers. Then the operation of loading began. This in itself invariably took half-an-hour, at the end of which time a bevy of porters and pages, varying in numbers, according to the size of the hotel, would cluster round for tips. On these occasions, Simon, to whom the mention of money is anathema, used to put his hand in his pocket and distribute, without looking at them, any scraps of paper that he might find, usually leaving the whole party destitute for the rest of the day.

It was therefore twenty minutes to twelve before we actually left the Potsdammerplatz. The first place of interest on the road was Wittenberg. The large open square in the middle of the town lined with high-fronted old houses, themselves dwarfed by the upstanding and irregularly-built Gothic cathedral, must look much the same now but for a statue or two commemorating the event, as when Luther flung the Papal Bull into the flames and started the Reformation on this identical spot four hundred and nine years ago. Simon tentatively suggested lunch; but David hurried through rather faster than usual, as though he were a practising Roman Catholic.

Though, as a matter of fact, he personally suffers from no form of religious hysteria, the way in which moral scruples can distort the actions of persons otherwise sane is sometimes scarcely believable. I have a relation who once sat eight hours without food or drink in a railway carriage at Monte Carlo on a boiling day in June, rather than set foot even on the platform of such a place. But then, after all, self-martyrdom is the greatest of all joys.

After driving some way further, the country began to assume an industrial complexion; but not as in England. This was no 'black country'. The grey and now more or less hedgeless panorama of small cultivated fields, relieved at intervals by rows of miniature Eiffel Towers bearing festoons of electric cable from one horizon to another, remained unchanged. Yet the inhabitants grew grimy, and a sudden wave of depression seemed to weight the air. The mining of coal and iron is all conducted in enormous craters two or three hundred feet below the surface of the fields. It is as though a peepshow designer had created a miniature replica of an industrial landscape at the bottom of a packing-case. Trucks and cranes and human beings can be seen moving vaguely about in miniature, like the people on the floor of St Paul's viewed through the hole in the floor of the ball. Then the fields continue again, until the next crater cleaves their midst.

As we drove by, the bands of workers on the road became ill-favoured and were at no pains to conceal their dislike of us, shaking their fists and shouting '*Langsam, langsam!*' (Slowly, slowly!) Germans always slow down to pass anything. David accelerates.

Though we had complained of the frequency with which the Hamburg-Berlin road had been closed for repairs, that indeed might have been an uncharted prairie compared with the present thoroughfare. Until at last, as Simon remarked, it was a comfort to be on a road at all, even if it was going in the wrong direction. One barrier necessitated a ten-mile detour along tracks that would have disgraced an Irish farm. David vowed he would make no further digressions into the countryside. Round the next corner stood the inevitable obstruction and its notice:

VORSICHT
GESPERRT.

A convenient field offered a way round. Then followed another obstacle, also circumventable. But the third was more formidable. A wooden pole was stretched across the road at a point where it was crossing a small valley on an embankment, so that on either side was a steep declivity. Below this barrier, which we removed, lay a row of stone blocks, heaped higgledy-piggledy on top of one another; and at one side an inflexible iron pin, eighteen inches high and one-and-a-half in diameter, was embedded deep into the roadway. We could move neither backward nor forward. A crowd collected from some neighbouring cottages, full of hostility. Suddenly David, without another moment's hesitation, charged the entire barricade. Bending the iron pin into a right-angle, Diana heaved her enormous body on to the stones and scattered them like the walls of Jericho. Simon and I rushed frantically in her wake, followed by the curses of the populace. Poised one on either step, we drove off in triumph.

At length we reached Leipzig, through long wastes of industrial suburbs. Simon, no longer tentative, insisted that we should have tea. David said that first we must find our way through the town. So we drove for half-an-hour through unending labyrinths of tramlined streets, and at last succeeded in coming out the other side, immediately beneath the grotesque stone *denkmal*, two hundred feet high, which was erected to commemorate the 'Battle of the Nations', the defeat that sent Napoleon to Elba – a shapeless mass resembling a squat chimney-stack built on the scale of the Great Pyramid. We also passed through the famous square where the allied troops were reviewed after the conflict.

Half a mile further on we ran into a bank backwards and doubled up the exhaust pipe, so that it now rent the ground with a loud tearing noise whenever Diana came down particularly heavily over any bump. Without a halt we continued our way to Altenburg, where we were obliged to stop, after seven hours uninterrupted driving, not for tea, but for petrol. This was Roumanian and unsatisfactory. The youth who filled the tank disliked us so much that he refused a tip. We passed through Plauen and stopped again to put on our coats.

As evening fell, the road led over the uplands; we were entering Bavaria. The flat country gave place to undulating hills covered with pinewoods, not of that familiar inky grey, but a lovely deep green, stretching away amongst yellow fields of corn and rich grassy valleys, till the blue horizon, still undulating, merged into a dull and misty lilac sunset. Gradually it became dark and we could smell the sweet scent of the pines that rose steep on either side as we whistled down the valleys; we could hear the trickle of streams; and could breathe the sharp fresh gusts of upland air as we climbed the hills again.

Bayreuth was but a pattern of lights. Simon hugged his stomach; I fell asleep. At half-past eleven we were on the Nuremberg tramlines when we again ran out of petrol. The spare tank was hauled from beneath the suitcases, a funnel formed of an *Illustrated London News,* and at twenty minutes to midnight, exactly twelve hours after leaving Berlin, we drew up outside the Hotel Palast-Fürstenhof, having touched neither food nor drink the whole day, and having made two stops of one and two minutes respectively.

We had a delicious meal of cold ham, poached eggs, and light beer brought up to our bedroom, and then slept soundly.

Nuremberg is the apotheosis of the tourist-town. There flourishes about her streets that kind of obvious antiquity, those over-ornamented crooked gables and twisted turrets, that appeal most strongly to those who love Age for its own sake, without being able to distinguish the textural beauty, and in some cases damage, that it can confer. It can be seen at a glance that these buildings are 'Old'. They shout Oldness. It needs no artistic acumen to tell that they were built without the aid of plumb-line and set-square. Nuremberg, in fact, is a place without atmosphere. Its main streets are lined with hotels and antique-shops and the buildings convey the same impression of affectation as the baronial rafters of the Queen's Hotel, Margate. After visiting the bank and being refused a cup of coffee at the 'Blue Bottle', we had lunch, and set out to drive the sixty-five miles to Rothenburg.

The Bavarian countryside is the most attractive in Central Europe. Rather than bewitching, it appears bewitched. Its mannerisms are those of the Albertian Christians. Santa Claus, who only visits other countries in the winter, makes this his home; and somehow, even in the bright August sunlight, with veitches and blue cranesbill growing from the long grass by the side of the narrow white roads, the idea seemed to have no incongruity about it. The villages and market towns consist of long twisted rows of white houses, sometimes frescoed with angels, which are drawn and tinted rather than painted. The roof of each house is half as high again as the side walls, and if old, it leans heavily towards its neighbour, or bellies the isosceles triangle of wall on which it rests out into the roadway. There is a fresh, clean atmosphere. The farmyard and the road are one, which makes motoring difficult. Little girls with tight, fair plaits scurry their flocks of geese out of the way. Bent and aged women, with brown, wrinkled faces peering from out their black handkerchiefs, may be seen going out in twos and threes to work in the fields. Everywhere the arms of the old kingdom are displayed, blue and white diagonal lozenges. In most of the villages are poles, a hundred feet or more high, which are striped round and round in blue and white and surmounted by a wreath hanging from the top. From these poles jut horizontal arms on which are placed innumerable painted, wooden toys, men on bicycles, motor cars, churches and animals.

On every second hill is perched a *schloss*, generally baroque, with a massive rounded tower or two surviving from an older fortress. Many of the *schlossen*, however, are situated in the middle of the towns, such as the enormous and very fine rococo palace at Ansbach, home of George II's queen. The Bavarian baroque is pleasant and not unwieldy, the churches being covered in a sort of yellow wash. Catholicism is very evident in the numerous shrines and figures of saints, in agitated stone draperies and iron halos, that guard the bridges on the road. Bavaria is the most German part of Germany; here all the 'Youth' movements originated, the country being especially suited to walking-tours. And it is here, more than in Prussia, that the survival of militarism is to be feared. The Crown Prince Rupprecht is still the most powerful man in the province. Monarchism will always evoke sympathy. But an independent Bavaria in her present frame of mind would not conduce to the peace of Europe.

Eventually, after taking a wrong turning out of Ansbach and being compelled to enquire the way of one of the witches of the field, we arrived at Rothenburg about four o'clock. This town surpasses belief. It is as though all the goblin haunts, palaces and fortress towers of fairyland were writhing in an elongated distortion glass; and yet, unlike those of Nuremberg, they ring true. There is a subtle distinction between the two towns. Both are visited by tourists, but Rothenberg by Germans only. Whereas Nuremberg is a conglomeration of all dates and styles, Rothenburg was built in the later Middle Ages and not a stone has been added or subtracted since. Her buildings are the more preposterous, but they do not suffer from that clustering ornamentation reminiscent of Burmese temples, with which the gables of Nuremberg are loaded. Rothenburg is a complete walled 'burg' of the Middle Ages. The walls have remained intact; at them, therefore, the town ends. In the fields beyond struggle one or two pink villas; that is all.

Entrance is effected through a series of gatehouses that are in themselves scarcely credible. From a central archway radiate two arc-shaped walls ending in a couple of round flanking turrets, with high-pitched, conical roofs. Over the actual gateway rises a tower, square in shape, and over sixty feet in height, up which runs a succession of little windows; while at the top, under the projecting eaves of a twisted and pagoda-like tiled roof, is a tiny house, having a row of these windows back and front, each embowered with a window-box. From one depends a string, on the end of which is a basket in which to haul up food. Here, surely, is a domicile reached only on a broomstick. In reality it is probably the dwelling of a neatly-dressed jeweller's assistant, newly married, who, owing to the housing shortage, is obliged to live either with his mother-in-law, or up 130 stairs.

The streets of the town shelve and twist like mountain paths. The roofs of the houses reach as high and half as high again as the walls on which they rest. Every window has its window-box, filled with geraniums, lobelia, and marguerites. At the end of the town furthest from the gate by which we entered, runs a street of magnificent old stone houses, into the front walls of which have been built, haphazard, the painted escutcheons of their former owners. One of these was erected by the Emperor Henry IV.

Groups of *Wandervögel*, with their bare necks and knees, were to be seen at every corner, making sketches. While David and Simon sat in a café, I also attempted, very unsuccessfully, to draw the town hall. Such, however, was the smell of the crowds of *Wandervögel* who insisted on looking over my shoulder, that I was eventually thankful to see Diana driving down the street to take me away.

Of all the fantastic, outlandish forms of medieval artistic expression that have come down to us, the Bavarian style of architecture is the most eccentric. That a perfect example of a complete town of the period should have survived in its entirety, unaltered, undemolished and unextended, in the heart of the country over which the Reformation and the counter-Reformation carried fire and sword, and the Thirty

Years War cannibalism and polygamy, is one of the miracles of history. Considering her absence of natural defences and the vicissitudes that she has endured, the phenomenon of Rothenburg's conservation is without parallel in Europe.

CHAPTER V

WHEN WE LEFT ENGLAND, the fashionable intelligentsia were all preparing their descent on Salzburg to attend the Mozart Festival, the production of which had been entrusted to M. Reinhardt. Either for the sake of their musical education, or simply for the purpose of meeting various friends, David and Simon had also decided to honour this feast in the musical calendar with their presence. In any case we left Nuremberg at half-past ten on Saturday morning for Austria.

David had arranged to lunch with a Hungarian baron, who, despite the fact that he himself possesses large estates in his own country and his wife in hers, which is Roumania, was spending the summer in Munich. Unfortunately we arrived an hour-and-a-half late, and he was gone. David telephoned his apologies to his mother. On the way we had had our first puncture, and had taken some time to change the wheel, as we were unable to find the jack. This had been strapped under the bonnet. Later, while travelling at sixty miles an hour down a very long stretch of straight road, a large white cock had stalked sedately out in front of us and emitted a sharp ping as we cut off his head with the front number-plate. At Ingolstadt we had crossed the Danube.

The main streets of Munich are magnificent. Their architecture is contemporary with that of the English Regency, the golden age of town planning. The architect who built them, under the auspices of King Ludwig, did not allow pediment and ornamental pillar to play so prominent a part in his design as in the English style, and favoured the purely Greek cornice ornamented with small upright acroteria in the shape of

oriental fans. It is to be hoped that the destinies of the city are
not ruled by a County Council and an Office of Works that
are intent on destroying any national monument that happens
to rest upon a lease.

We lunched, half fainting, at the best hotel, and had a ham
omelette and some Rhine wine.

We left at about three o'clock and began ascending the
mountains, eventually coming down on Wasserburg, which
resembles from above a miniature Venice, being situated on
several islands in the middle of the Inn, which here broadens
to the dimensions of a small lake. We had reached the very
centre of the town, when another puncture occurred beneath
the spreading trees of a little triangular green. The whole
population poured out like an audience from a burning cinema,
until we were encircled by a pushing, chattering crowd, which
pressed so close that it was impossible to turn the jack or fix
the wheel without jolting some inquisitively bent bare knee
that might have seen anything from two to eighty summers.

From Wasserburg we ascended steadily, and the cottages and
churches developed eaves and onion domelets in the Austro-
Swiss manner. A mile from the frontier the petrol gave out.
Recourse was had to the spare tank; and the suitcases, books,
and hats were strewn all over the neighbouring fields in our
enraged efforts to unearth it. At this moment another car
appeared. Alarmed at the scene of wreckage, it stopped to
enquire and stayed to chat. The driver, enveloped like the rest of
his party in a white dust sheet, said that his name was Tomaselli.
He commended us by note to the proprietor of the Hotel de
l'Europe, where, we told him, we had engaged rooms. David
believed him to be a famous Italian singer; while I had an idea
that he was a well-known racing motorist. It turned out that he
kept a café in Salzburg. The proprietor was rather sniffy.

At the frontiers, which were divided by a wooden bridge that
spanned a rushing river, we were obliged to wait an hour, while
David attempted to argue back the exorbitant deposit that he
had paid on the two spare outer covers at Hamburg. The head

official then discovered that there was not enough money in the office to meet the demand. He promised to have it ready on Monday. Meanwhile Simon and I walked backwards and forwards over the heavy wooden planks of the bridge. There is something absurd about a land frontier. The guards seemed to know all the local residents as they walked across the bridge driving animals, or on their way to visit friends. The Austrian *douanier* was at a village dance and had to be fetched. He was so anxious to return that he did not examine our trunks, though astonished at their quantity. We assured him that they contained nothing but clothes.

The first thing that we were told on at last reaching Salzburg was that the Festival did not begin until Wednesday. David was furious, Simon indifferent. Personally, after driving six hundred and fifty miles in the last three days I looked forward to a quiet weekend.

That evening after dinner, we went out into the garden and watched some dancing on a tiled floor laid down beneath the trees, from which depended large and unbecoming electric light bulbs. The band was not expert, and the atmosphere not unlike that of a provincial palais-de-danse on a Monday afternoon.

The next morning we were awakened by the incessant shunting of trams at the station over the road, varied by the strains of a numerous brass band, which paraded the streets with sabbatarian exuberance from 9 till 12. David turned over and went to sleep. Seizing sketch book and pencil, I rose out of bed, and seating myself on the balcony, revenged myself on Salzburg with an uncomplimentary drawing of the station and one factory chimney.

The remainder of our Sunday we spent in the conventional manner. During the afternoon Simon and I wrote letters to our mothers; and later, when the heat had abated, we set out for our Sabbath walk. We had intended scaling one of the mountains with which the town is oppressively overhung. The hotel advised us to take a tram to Plazl for this purpose. We did so, and it set us down in the middle of the town, by the river. Passing through an archway we began the ascent of a steep and rocky footpath, on the right-hand side of which, set back in wire-faced grottos cut out of the cliff, were twelve life-size 'Stations of the Cross' in hideously realistic painted plaster. The path continued, until we were suddenly confronted by a wooden door labelled in Gothic 'Mozart's House'. Turning back precipitately, we wandered disconsolately about the suburbs in company with many others – courting couples, happy families, and grand-dads and -dams. It was still extraordinarily hot. Persevering, we reached the country, and giving up the idea of mountains, sank into a primitive beer-garden. The inn-keeper, in shorts and a Tyrolese hat, was talking to a friend, in the same costume, smoking a long and curly German pipe. Two or three Alsatians loafed about, free from their daily labour of drawing little hand-carts. A buxom gal brought us beer and was forced to accept our German money in payment. We sat beneath a chestnut tree and felt very happy. Then we walked home. Simon, in neat plus fours and loud chocolate-and-white stockings, was an object of admiration. The plus four has 'caught on' in Germany and Austria, and bank clerks wear it.

That evening we again watched the dancing in the garden. It was enlivened by a Viennese waltz, to which everyone danced the old six step with a little hop in the middle – all except one exclusive party who sat ostentatiously aloof until the next fox-trot. This party contained amongst others a handsome old man in a white moustache, who was referred to as the Baron, and an extremely good-looking woman, with copper, shingled hair, and a tight-fitting dress of red and gold. In my eyes, however, their pre-eminence in the world of fashion was dissolved when next day I found the woman's portrait peering slyly from the window of the local photographer.

On Monday morning I visited the cathedral and also an unusual Gothic church supported by high, thin, round pillars like factory chimneys; then breakfasted in the Residenzplatz.

This is a large open space with an elaborate fountain in the middle; to one side is the Residenz, a long, creamy and very simple baroque building with an archway in the middle; on another the cathedral; and flanking it, a tall tower and a shady row of chestnut trees. From the former there suddenly issued a melancholy, quavering old tune, wafted on the hot, still air by an ancient peal of bells. Everyone showed great interest and looked up, though there was nothing to see. This was followed by an organ recital in the cathedral, where I was able to get cool, until two enormous women, smelling of dentifrice, came and sat down on top of me. On the way back David picked me up in the car.

After lunch we left for Innsbruck. Though both Innsbruck and. Salzburg are in Austria, the geographical vagaries of the district make it necessary to pass over a tongue of Germany if a hundred-mile detour is to be avoided. This meant, therefore, returning along the road by which we had come and crossing four separate frontier barriers. Naturally the money equivalent to the Hamburg deposit, promised on Saturday night, was not ready, and there was a delay while it was fetched. During this we talked to one of the German guards. He said that he had been in prison for three-and-a-half years at Dorchester. It was a source of tremendous pleasure to him to talk about it. He had had to work; the English were good fighters in the trenches; it was all over now, and must never happen again. He spoke not a word of English. The Austrian sentries wear khaki, the Germans bottle-green.

We passed at first through gigantic mountains. The road wound up their pine-covered declivities, until it was impossible to look over the side of the car without feeling dizzy. The colours were attractive, though not beautiful; very rich green grass fields, usually perpendicular, on which could be seen men hanging by one hand and reaping with the other; then the pine-woods, a deeper, blacker green; and at the top, great white faces of rock stretching up into the blue sky, very little of which was visible. Some of the summits were snow-covered.

The fact that this was the Tyrol was emphasised by a special local customs barrier, which charged a pound to let Diana enter the province. The delay enabled us to have a drink of soda water.

We reached Innsbruck as it was growing misty. The town lies at the foot of enormous mountains. It is uninteresting and almost squalid, catering for native as much as foreign tourists. It has the same atmosphere of bustling trippers as Keswick, the centre of the English mountain district.

The hotel, the Tyrolerhof, smelt strongly of rice pudding, and was adorned with clocks under glass shades. After a long, late dinner, we were sitting half asleep in the reading-room, when it was invaded by some forty American women, each one with a voice like a surgical knife, accompanied by two men and a boy. While I was reaching for my spectacles which were on the table, a member of the party neatly slipped herself in between my upraised knees and the seat of my armchair. She was middle-aged with a strong, efficient face, and had had, I hope, an unhappy married life. She wore a toque adorned with flattened pansies. The men proceeded to make speeches, setting forth the course of action for the morrow, like Roman generals 'exhorting' their troops. As the ceremony continued, we laughed so much that we had to retire. A woman had sat next to us at dinner in a dress of cheap, brown tussore, printed with green and yellow boxes in perspective, so that she might have been covered with angular warts. These danced before my eyes long into the night.

CHAPTER VI

THE DAY OF OUR DEPARTURE from Innsbruck was to prove the most harassing twelve hours of the whole tour. It was only the persistence of David, who argued without ceasing in French and German from twelve o'clock midday until eight at night, that prevented the complete collapse of all our plans.

An hour's driving brought us to the Italian frontier. The road ascended the mountains in a series of alarming bends, each of which disclosed a drop of five hundred to a thousand feet as we skidded round the outside edge. However, we reached the Brenner Pass, four thousand feet up, without changing gear. Here it was as pleasantly cool as Innsbruck had been hot and dusty. Earlier in the morning I had visited the cathedral and purchased a belt. Unfortunately this was incapable of refined adjustment, and it threatened either to cut me in half or let my trousers drop to the knee.

The Austrian barrier was passed with little difficulty. We drove brightly across the 100 yards of no-man's land and stopped before the Italian. Here was a great to-do. A very new marble monument, about the size of a pillar-box, enclosed in a quadrangle of railings, proclaimed that this was now Italy. Upon its face was the following inscription:

Q.B.F.F.F.S.
Italiae et
Austriae
Terminus
Sangermanensi
Foedere

Consecratus
X. IX. MCMXIX.

Further on stood an enlarged *chalet,* festooned with green, white and red flags. The pole across the road was painted in similar colours. And two upstanding flagstaffs wafted their triumphant nationalism from mounds on either side of it.

The customs men in their grey-green uniforms and Robin Hood hats, small, surly and very dirty, contrasted strongly with the benign Austrians, who still stood looking after us from the threshold of their office door. Our passports having been examined, one of the officials stepped on board and we drove through the barrier and down to the customs house, which was at the railway station on the left of the road. There was a train in at the time and we had to wait our turn. I changed my kronen into lire and Simon and I drank two pennyworth of red wine in the third-class waiting-room. Everyone to whom we spoke a syllable of Italian answered in German, and vice versa.

Suddenly we saw David hurrying towards us. They were refusing to let us pass without paying the full deposit on the car – in the neighbourhood of four hundred pounds. The reason was that the preliminary declaration by the customs of the country of origin had not been filled in. This was the fault of the leaden-headed official who had arrived two hours late at Grimsby. We all three returned to the breach; but it was useless. The man waved his printed instructions in our faces. We left the office, and jumping into Diana, raced back to the barrier on bottom gear, making a great deal of noise to show our annoyance. The sentries seemed to resent such peculiar behaviour, as if our return were due simply to English eccentricity. They re-stamped our passports, and we passed on to the Austrian barrier, still on bottom gear, although the road sloped downhill. We were in despair. All our letters and the Greek *laissez-passer* were waiting in Rome; and here we were apparently condemned either to return to England or remain north of the Alps for ever.

The Austrians, however, took a different view. Declining to reduce their books and our passports to confusion, they ridiculed the Italians and their tawdry frontier decorations flapping in the wind a hundred yards up the valley.

'Since they've come this side of the mountains they've been above themselves,' they said – Austrian interests having suffered considerably in the Brenner district when the northern frontiers were revised. And so, in revenge for the Great War, the Austrians, with complete irrelevance, plastered their stamps and signatures on the *Carnet* in the place of the missing Grimsby declaration.

Much amused we crossed the strip of neutral territory once more. This time the Italians made no attempt to conceal their disgust at our reappearance. For the third time they befouled our passports and their own registers, and with the same official on board we drove down to the customs once again. The officer was not deceived; nor was he amused. He insisted that we must have the English voucher.

Could we telephone to the embassy at Rome, we asked?

Certainly; if he received orders from his finance minister to let us through, he would do so. The Embassy could no doubt make the necessary arrangements. Meanwhile, we must move the car back again behind the barrier.

To this last request David would not accede; and taking Simon, who hates scenes, by the arm, he walked up the road to the *chalet*, which combined the functions of public house, post-office and barracks, to telephone. I remained in the car.

A crowd of gesticulating little men gathered round, beseeching, commanding, cursing, whining and growling: the car must be taken back. I explained that I could not drive it. That made no difference. They produced a porter with a dropped lower lip who spoke almost less English than I Italian. The babel continued, until at length, bored, and unable to cope with their torrents of prayer and abuse, I produced my sketch-book, harpened my pencil with an expensive-looking knife, the property of Simon, and with exasperating deliberation proceeded to depict with meticulous care a group of pine trees that sprang from a hillock near the station. This infuriated them and they tried to snatch the book away, with the result that my pencil shot across the sky in a jagged curve that could not even have passed muster as a telegraph wire. My blood boiled in its turn. The porter being the ostensible excuse for using English, I rose to my feet and shouted so that crowds more came running out of the station. I roared that I could not drive the car, and that if I could, I should refuse; that I was not going to fetch my friends; and that I had not come half across Europe in three days to be ordered about by them.

Without understanding a word they fell back, and David arid Simon returned to find me in peaceful possession. The post-mistress was at lunch.

Our midday meal we had brought with us in a bag. This we now ate in the post-office. Since the drive to Nuremberg, Simon had become wary and had insisted on the hotels supplying us with ham rolls. In spite of them he was miserable, cowed by the officialdom that David and I delighted to defy: he threatened to take the next train that passed through the station, wherever it went. We suggested that he should go to Rome for help. He said that he did not wish to arrive there in flannel trousers. Eventually, despite the assurances of the post-mistress that it was impossible, we got through on the telephone to the capital, but found that the Embassy was shut; it would not be open until five. Our difficulties were considerable, as I knew only a very little Italian, the others none, and the post-mistress equally little German.

At five we telephoned again, but this time were unable to get through. So, in desperation, we drafted a tear-stained telegraphic appeal to the ambassador, invoking any wife's-sister's-mother-in-law's-cat connections of the foreign office with whom we could claim the smallest acquaintance, begging him to insist on the finance minister's despatching immediate instructions to the Brenner authorities to let us pass. We settled down to await events.

The inn displayed further evidences of the Italian pride of conquest. The word *Gasthof*, with which it was originally labelled, had been, crossed out and *Albergo* painted by its side. Similarly, *Sala di Pranza* had been substituted for *Essenzimmer*. The soldiers were singing opera in hideous tones from the upper windows, from which their clothes were hanging out to dry. We began to hate the Italians. Everything seemed to irritate. A tablet on the outside wall recording the fact that Goethe had once laid his head upon a pillow in this very building increased our detestation of philosophy.

While we were thus pawing the ground, exacerbated almost beyond endurance, there arrived in this remote corner of Europe a certain officer of the Life Guards who once incensed the cheaper press by striking a policeman with the flat of his sword for not saluting the colours. The Life Guards are, it is said, more amusing than other regiments. The policeman at the time was holding up the traffic with one hand and directing it with the other.

At length David, goaded by the disappearing back view of the interloper, determined to make one more attempt to argue us through. The altercation lasted three hours in as many languages. We became so persistent that we were eventually ushered before the Chief. He pointed to the instructions on the *Carnet*, printed in every known language; he was helpless. Then David, who does not understand a word of Italian, drew a bow at a venture; he pretended to find a loophole in the Italian version, in the absence of a certain defining phrase that qualified the French and German. This idea seemed to have its effect upon the official. We pressed the point for half an hour; and at last, weary of our pertinacity, which threatened to keep him at his desk all night, he consented to risk his job, his life, his all, and let us pass. After another hour's wait for a train, during which we drank our rejoicings in thick smoky *chianti* in the waiting-room, he signed the paper; we filed into the car; and amid torrents of rain, with the clouds obscuring the whole valley, we sped jubilantly down the road into Italy.

Darkness fell just in time to prevent our catching a glimpse of the Dolomites.

The tension and worry of the day had left us exhausted. We passed through many villages, in which the headlights flashed on German names above the shop windows, relieved occasionally by the Royal Italian Arms displayed over a post-office or on a flag.

We reached Bolzano at nine o'clock for dinner. The hotels did not look attractive and David drove straight through to Trento, another hour's run, during which Simon and I slept. There we ate *hors d'oeuvres* and a ham omelette. David, who, in Germany, had never ceased telling us how he could not touch Italian food, busily licked every platter dry. At eleven o'clock we set out for Verona. At twelve we had a puncture in the narrow and now silent streets of Rovereto, to the astonishment of two old women who were sitting quietly talking at their front doors, when an enormous car drew up, blocking the whole of the street, and began to take itself to pieces at their feet. We reached Verona about half-past one, and had great difficulty in finding the hotel and awakening it.

The heat was intense and the rooms small and stuffy. Each grasping a bottle of mineral water, we fell into bed, scarcely able to undress. The mattresses were made of stone; the beds of tin, on which were painted sprays of roses and landscapes. But we slept the sleep of utter fatigue, and did not wake up until the sun began to pierce the green shutters of our windows late next morning.

CHAPTER VII

IN A BOOK named *Up and Down,* E.F. Benson, its author, describes the sensation of 'coming home' that always assails him on his entry into Italy. What is it that arouses this emotion in English people, in men and women who have not a drop of foreign blood in their veins? An emotion that, far from being the result of habit, can only be stirred to the full by the initial rapture of the first arrival, of the first vision of the cypresses and campaniles, the hummock-borne fortress towns of Umbria, the wild stretches of the Campagna and the ultimate incarnation of Vesuvius and her stone-pine? What is it? Do all nationalities experience this conviction that Italy is their birthright, just as great works of art are the heritage of civilization? Or is there a something akin between the island and the peninsula, a something not similar, but which by reason of its very distinction from the rest of Europe, constitutes an affinity? It may be a quality too subtle for definition. But the fact remains, English people live in Italy because, unlike the Riviera and apart from the artistic monuments, they can love the country as a home. In France the resorts become Anglicised; in Italy the visitors Italianised. The English resident is not liked; but in his sincerity must be sought his absolution from the charge of 'living cheaply on the natives'. He loves the country.

Thus it was with this inevitable exhilaration that I left the hotel on the morning of my third arrival in Italy and turning a corner, entered the market place of Verona, a large square, flooded with huge flapping white umbrellas, under which stood stalls of fruit and flowers and other necessaries. I drank a cup of coffee and bought myself a buttonhole; Simon then appeared. We decided to stay another night. He was interested, as he had not visited Italy before.

Verona shows strong traces of the Venetian domination. The windows of the older palaces are built in that form of graceful Gothic arcading, so beautiful in its legitimate setting of delicate unrelieved brick, so repellent as popularised by Ruskin amid the walls of the miniature Chantillys and Rambouillets with which he decorated the cities where his influence was paramount. Weatherbeaten lions of St Mark are to be seen prowling above the doors of the municipal buildings; and the towers are roofed with those foursided cones that are peculiar to the north-east corner of the country.

At the back of the hotel, in a little courtyard attendant on a small and very ancient church, we came upon the tombs of the della Scala family. Of the three most important, each is surmounted by an elaborate Gothic *baldochino*, some twenty-five feet high, on top of which is perched an equestrian statue. The finest of these, that of Can Grande, is an exceptional work of art that can only be compared with the equestrian fresco in the Palazzo Publico, at Siena, by Simone Martini. The horses in both are draped to the fetlock; and there is something unusual, and at the same time satisfying, in the implied movement of an animal beneath the conventional but now unfamiliar folds of formal drapery. The riders, too, communicate something of their complacency to the beholder.

The courtyard is enclosed by a low wall, on top of which is stretched a kind of gigantic wrought-iron chain mail, introducing into its design the family badge, the ladder. Though dating from the fourteenth century, it is still as flexible as a gold purse. Verona has adopted the ladder as her badge; it appeared in blue and orange on the stained-glass windows of the hotel.

A guide, who spoke French, showed us round the tombs. He then pointed to three windows in an overlooking palace, and said that behind them Danté had composed the *Divina*

Commedia. Moving his podgy forefinger a few degrees further round the compass, he fixed upon a low red-brick shell of a house, the ground-floor of which was occupied by a wheelwright's shop. This, he said, was the palace of Romeo's family, where Romeo had actually lived. There is always a certain unreasonable humour about the reverence that foreigners display for Shakespeare. Simon and I burst into unthinking merriment, at which the guide took great offence. He angrily spluttered out long passages of Danté, which were intended to prove that Romeo's family was not merely an ornament of fiction, and that if it had been, it had existed not only in the imagination of our national poet, but also in that of his.

After lunch we motored to Vicenza, twenty miles east across the Lombardy plain. It was very hot; the white dust was stifling and the road monotonous. Vicenza was the home of Palladio, for whose works, as the founder of English domestic architecture, David had a peculiar reverence. He does not admit the Jacobean and Elizabethan styles to be architecture. The Gothic town hall, re-encased by the master in a light, silver-grey stone that has not lost its freshness, is a lovely building, though it presents the appearance of an inverted galleon. There were one or two other fragments to be seen. Palladio's sense of proportion was unfailing, and it is this, whether we owe it to him or not, that is the outstanding characteristic of the late seventeenth and eighteenth century English country house.

That evening, after an early dinner, we had the satisfaction of feeling that we had at last been fully compensated for anything that we might have missed at the Mozart Festival. I cannot do better than quote the column that appeared a fortnight later in the *Times* of August 29th:

ROSSINI'S 'MOSES'
PERFORMANCE IN THE VERONA ARENA
(From a Correspondent)

…a performance more astounding and grandiose than could have been expected even of Italy. Mozart and M. Reinhardt faded into insignificance. The elements themselves were harnessed to this production.

The opera was Rossini's 'Mosé'; the theatre the famous 'Arena'. This enormous Roman amphitheatre, the most complete of its kind in the world, presented an astonishing appearance. From the further section of the vast arena a row of brilliant electric lamps, so dazzling as to fulfil the functions of a curtain, proclaimed the existence of a stage fifty yards in length. This was flanked by two towering, white obelisks, against which could vaguely be discerned two lesser dark ones. An immense chatter filled the night, as the tiers and tiers of people loomed up to the black roof of sky. To one side, high up above the whole, three ruined arches, outlined faintly light against the firmament, stood symbol of the past. Reminder of the present, a lively overture burst out, to be drowned beneath the storm of hisses with which each member of the audience thought fit to admonish his neighbour to silence. Then suddenly, amid the clash of cymbals the row of electric lights reversed, beams shone from the smaller obelisks, and the twelve tribes of Israel, arrayed with all the picturesqueness of a missionary calendar, were disclosed in a tremendous concourse against a jungle of luxuriant vegetation and a great mass of overhanging rocks and boulders.

Irrelevant as the detail may have been – for instance, two pompous, Renaissance equestrian statues prancing among the palms behind the obelisks – it was an impressive spectacle by reason of its very size and the very sound emitted by this colossal chorus. At length there came a pause – a roll of drums, a crash – and, with a superb gesture, Moses stepped out upon a promontory of rock. He was 'after Michael Angelo': a tremendous figure of a man with a far-reaching bass voice; his hair twisted into horns, his beard flowing down in the traditional ringlets of the famous statue, as though each strand were musclebound. Throughout, a pillar of power and strength, he dominated the performance as he dominated the Israelites.

The chronology of the opera is curious. The first act is occupied with the giving of the tables. While Aaron struggled with the people in an acquiescent tenor, darkness fell upon the stage, save for one spot illuminated by a prism of light. The orchestra quickened. Lightning flashed from the wings, to be answered by summer lightning, shot in violet streaks across the sky. The Almighty, a baritone, spake. Then, with a blare of trumpets, the Prophet stood forth bearing the tables. The act ended with a tremendous finale, and the audience shouted for Moses, and shouted again. He eventually reappeared with only his horns emerging from a gargantuan laurel wreath adorned with false berries and upheld by two black-shirted Fascisti. These blandly arrogated to themselves the thunders of applause that greeted the trio.

It lasted from nine till one. The Italians take their national composers very seriously. In the third act, unnerved by the stupendous bad taste with which modern imagination has invested the courts of ancient Egypt, the leading tenor missed his note – and the populace burst into a tumult of loathing and disapprobation. The last scene, however, was superb. The lights reversed, disclosing, as at the beginning, the people of Israel, in a long and sombre line. Behind them, instead of jungle growths, the Red Sea heaved and rolled in a manner ominously uncalm. Led by Moses, a figure scarcely human in the growing twilight, the tribes sang a protracted and mournful farewell song. Above, the summer lightning flashed, accompanied now by distant rumbles of thunder. Then the inevitable followed. Pharaoh and his host were espied in pursuit. With a supreme gesture Moses turned upon the waters, harangued them, hypnotized them, and slowly watched them part. Soon only a diagonal stream of heads was visible between the waves. As the last disappeared, Pharaoh sprang to view, a sinister silhouette perched high upon a rock.

A short recitative of hate ensued. The thunder – natural, not orchestral – drew nearer. Followed by his army he rushed in the wake of the fugitives. Like doom the waters bore down upon them, closed and resumed their inexorable rolling, punctuated for a minute by an occasional arm or spear waving in awful despair. The orchestra grew calmer. A great red sun appeared on an infinitely distant black cloth and spread the rays of hope over the waters. Then all was over.

It had been an astonishing performance. The very scale on which it was produced ensured its success. And the advent of real thunder and lightning to synchronise with the wrath of Pharaoh produced a dramatic effect which may never be repeated. During the intervals we drank beer and vermouth and ate composite ices in the vaulted crypt that ran round beneath the tiers of seats, where formerly lions and Christians had awaited their turn to gratify the frivolity of the public. And now, upon this very site, that in days gone by was wont to parade the pagan orgies of a corrupting empire, a representation of the most treasured of all our Old Testament stories was actually in progress. Such, my brethren, are the miracles that Faith has wrought.

CHAPTER VIII

AS WE WALKED BACK FROM THE OPERA, David said that we ought to start for Florence at 10 o'clock the next morning. Supposing that, as usual, he meant twelve, I lay in bed until the porter suddenly came up for my luggage. My toilet was therefore necessarily hurried, and I started the day in a state of disorder.

Motoring down the plain of Lombardy is not interesting. The roads are passably smooth and wide, but so dusty that even a horse and cart throws up a cloud that obscures the view for ten to twenty yards; while a preceding motor vehicle makes it impossible to see for half-a-mile. One is seldom out of sight of a house. Villas large and small, former homes of the Medici and residences of local bank managers, lie always a quarter-of-a-mile, or not so far, off the road, visible at the end of perfectly straight avenues, through pairs of elaborate and pompous gate-posts. Every vineyard can boast an entrance which in England would denote a substantial mansion of the Georgian period. The country is entirely cultivated in strips, that are, like everything else, at right angles to the road. Though the plain is completely flat, it is impossible to see anything in the late summer owing to tall crops of maize and other unfamiliar growths, and the festoons of vines hanging from the rows of little pollarded trees. The loads of hay are even bigger than in Germany, being piled right on to the horse's back so that only the ears of the animal remain visible. As David is never intimidated into removing his foot from the accelerator by any substance so fragile as grass, we generally carried off about a third of a rick from each load that we passed. Simon, seated on the left outside, was apt to receive most of it on his head. For a person who prides himself on his manners, he was in a false position.

We passed through Villafranca, interesting only for its strip of tarred road, and crossed the Po, entering Mantua by a covered bridge. The pandemonium in this narrow, darkened tunnel was indescribable. Long lines of carts and droves of unmanageable cattle, panic-stricken by the reverberating echoes, jostled from side to side in angry confusion. We reached Bologna about midday, and, after driving three times round the town in search of the Restaurant Grande Italia, lunched at the Hotel Baglioni. Italian food at its best can compare with any in the world; and the Grande Italia had had the reputation of being the finest restaurant in Italy. Though now closed, its mantle seemed to have fallen on the Baglioni, which also contained an excellent American Bar, run by a waiter trained at the Savoy.

It was four o'clock before we eventually started out for Florence again, feeling very lazy and looking forward to arriving there. Five hours later we made an ignominious re-entry into Bologna, attached to the end of a rope.

Our first misfortune was to take the wrong road out of the town, which, after about five miles, lured us without warning into the midst of a group of smaller Apennines, mountains which in reality are just as preposterous as they appear in Perugino backgrounds, and not, therefore, as a rule, frequented by motorists. Up and up we twisted round these amusement-park peaks by a track not an inch wider than the wheel-base of the car, and so steep that the luggage nearly fell out of the back; round corners that Diana's huge body could scarcely negotiate without her hind wheels flying into mid-air three hundred feet above some smiling farmstead; down valleys so narrow that she bridged them; and up humps so sharp that they threatened to harpoon her undercarriage; all this far up in the heavens with a view of fifty miles on either side. Having forced a passage through a cemetery, we felt, when the road threatened to pass through the front door of a farm, that the

moment had arrived to turn round. And we had at least on
the way back, the satisfaction of finding that another car had
followed us and was now stuck in the cemetery, its occupants
goggled and hooded, gesticulating among the tombs. We left
them silhouetted against the skyline, looking like a party of
divers stranded on a mountain peak.

Turning a corner we suddenly found ourselves sliding down
a precipice, tilted so far forward that it was necessary to hold
ourselves back with our hands pressed against the dashboard
as half-a-dozen Apennine valleys beckoned invitingly below.
Ramming the gears to the lowest and putting on both brakes,
David could just hold the car as we slithered down what was
little better than a goat-run. Once at the bottom we hurried
along to rejoin the main road and landed in a dried river-bed.
Backing, we fell into a ditch. Luckily a large stone caught the
rear off-wheel. Eventually we shot out of it, dragging with us
the stone and about a hundredweight of earth. When at last
we did attain the main road, we had not gone a hundred yards
along it, when for no conceivable reason, Diana came to a
sudden and irrevocable standstill.

David thought that the root of the trouble must be the
carburettor. So did I. Simon did not venture an opinion.
After unloading our combined luggage in an effort to find the
book of instructions which all the time was safely in the front
locker where it should have been, we set about the carburettor
with spanners and pincers; and after an hour's hard work
succeeded in getting it in pieces. There seemed nothing
the matter; we blew the jets at either end until our cheeks
ached; then put it together again. After that we changed the
plugs, because they 'wanted doing anyhow'. This made no
difference. It was useless. We gave up in despair and decided
to stop a car and ask for help. Every five minutes for the last
two hours we had been so enveloped in dust by mechanically
driven transport, as to be scarcely able to breathe. But now,
in the natural course of things, another hour elapsed before
anything appeared at all.

At last, from round the corner of the bridge down the road, came the rumble of a lorry. With arms outstretched, like the little girl on the railway line, we stopped it, and two beneficent and filthy human beings, with immensely round stomachs concealed beneath white aprons, emerged from the front. They fastened on Diana's inside with the ecstasy of starving leeches. In a moment the engine was emitting sheets of flame. David reached between the licking tongues and turned off the petrol; Simon and I scooped the refuse of the gutter into Diana's most delicate intestines; and, while one of the men thrust his enormous torso bodily on top of the carburettor, the other fetched a piece of sacking from the lorry, with which ne eventually quenched the conflagration.

Laughing loudly, the men then embarked on a second attempt, this time wrapping the sacking round the carburettor in the first instance. We remained more collected, with one eye on the luggage at the back, as the flames shot up in the air. Finally they tried a third time. But it was not a success. They decided to tow us.

I sat in front off the lorry with the larger of the two. He started off with a bound that snapped the rope like a piece of thread. We retied it and tried again. The lorry was delivering Bolzano beer, with the result that we stopped at every public house on the road proving a refreshing object of ridicule to the parties of drinkers seated barefooted and half hidden in the dust. My companion told me that he had a son who spoke German and English. He also made a great deal of other conversation which I did not understand, occasionally almost stopping to apostrophise the landscape. The other man danced about the back of the lorry, asking David and Simon if he could introduce them to any ladies.

Our progress was slow, and it was nearly dark by the time we reached the tram terminus, which lay some distance out in the country. The lorry could delay no longer. Explaining our plight to the occupant of the Bologna Tramways Office, our two benefactors left us, they to deliver the remainder of their beer, we to telephone to the Baglioni for assistance. Though not easy, we succeeded in getting through. Another car would arrive in about half-an-hour.

During the interval we entered a wineshop. Two *Wandervögel* were eating bread and milk at a neighbouring table. A kitten with a dislocated shoulder proved an object of interest and affection to David. The car arrived, accompanied by an interpreter, who resembled Harold Lloyd in mind and face, confusing every issue that he was called upon to solve. The rope broke again. We mended it and reached the hotel about nine, three ghoulish figures, unrecognisable beneath a livid coating of clotted, white dust. Baths and dinner revived us. The waiter expressed himself willing, if necessary, to introduce us to some ladies. Instead we went out and entered the first café that we came to.

Being rather tired we sat for some time in silence. The waiter behind the counter showed great interest in us. Eventually, handing me a confidential vermouth, he suggested that we might care to meet some ladies. Meanwhile his mother, a plump and elderly woman behind a pay desk, with clay-white skin and a wicked gleam in her eyes that belied her benevolent smile, was whispering in David's ear that she did, as a matter of fact, know of some ladies who would not be unwilling to make our acquaintance. As an alternative she produced with furtive secrecy one of those packs of ' greasy' playing cards that one had imagined existed only among gold-diggers and pirates, and with these she tried to wave us into the back premises. Other people seemed to be coming and going in a mysterious way. The atmosphere became so disreputable that we began to feel uncomfortable.

Meanwhile we had made friends with a small Fascista, who spoke French. He was extremely communicative. He was a private – as opposed to an official – policeman; that is to say, a night-watchman. Despite this he was always about in the day. That morning, in fact, his father, who was a policeman proper, had been taken ill; and he had himself donned the livery and cocked hat of the House of Savoy and gone out to do duty instead. Bologna was a charming town. Yes, he thought it might be possible for us to join the local Fascisti. If we would come with him tomorrow morning he would see what could be done. Meanwhile, if we would like the meet any ladies, there would be no difficulty. And he and the waiter and the waiter's mother all fell into an earnest and unintelligible conversation. We thought it time to escape.

In order to spare the reader the suspense and irritation, aggravated by the intense heat and airlessness of the town, that we ourselves endured, it may be as well to admit that our stay in Bologna was prolonged to the extent of six days. On the morning after the disaster, It was discovered that one of the cog-wheels in the magneto had been stripped of its teeth. The car would be ready on Saturday. But the peculiarities of the 'distribution' made it impossible to fit a foreign magneto. It was therefore necessary to remake the inside of the old one. Saturday was a holiday, on which the mechanics could not work; Sunday was a Sunday, on which they could. The presence in the town of a 'State Magneto Works' facilitated matters to a certain extent. The car would be ready on Monday night. Meanwhile, if we were lonely, the mechanic would be delighted to effect a meeting between ourselves and some ladies who were friends of his.

To cut a long story short, the car was not in fact in running order until Wednesday evening. As David had particularly enquired, before leaving England whether it would be advisable to take a spare magneto, and had been met with a distinct negative from the firm from whom he had purchased the car, we felt that our annoyance was justifiable. At the same time we obtained an insight into certain aspects of Italian provincial life that is not vouchsafed to everyone.

CHAPTER IX

BOLOGNA IS A LARGE MANUFACTURING TOWN containing 280,000 inhabitants. Famous in the Middle Ages for her resistance to papal encroachment, she has retained this independence of attitude with regard to the puritan elements of Fascismo. In Florence, but a fortnight before our arrival, an American woman had been brought into court for kissing in the street, and had only with difficulty been rescued by her consul from a term of imprisonment. In Bologna there is no need to kiss in the street. Whether or not it is due to the combined excesses of a barracks and a university, the town is famed as a seminary of temptation, a fount of loose-living, whence tributaries flow into all the other cities of Italy. Oddly enough, however, the inhabitants are never in bed. At one in the morning the cafés are as full as at midday. At two, they close. At four they re-open. This is in extreme contrast to most Italian cities, which invariably present, after midnight, an empty and subdued appearance.

But the main feature of Bologna is her arcades. Not only the streets in the centre of the town, but the side streets and the slum streets, are all arcaded. The fronts of the houses rest on every imaginable kind of arch, pillar and capital, Gothic and Classic. Thus it is possible to walk always in the shade and always under cover. The effect is one of strong shadows and bright arcs of light; while at night the pale glimmer of the street lamps flits in long streaks up the everlasting corridors, thick with the undispersed heat of the molten August day. And everywhere the echoes resound as in a huge subdued swimming-bath, to heighten the chatter and hubbub of the cafés, and accentuate the solitary footstep of an errant girl, or the bang of a door and the rattle of a chain.

Though the opinions of others on the subject of hotels are tedious, the Baglioni deserves record as in our opinion the best in Italy. The food, which made no cosmopolitan pretences, showed to what heights Italian food could rise. The staff were attentive and polite, and the management offered to change our English cheques when the banks were shut. Finally our bill was not excessive. The building had been once an old palace, and the frescoed vaulting of the dining-room was still intact. This had been the work of one of the brothers Caracci, natives of the city, executed in that same late Roman style of design adopted by Raphael in the famous loggia at the Vatican.

We ourselves were lodged in an annexe, also a former palace, with a staircase of grandiose proportions adorned with white and gold urns and rams' heads. At the top was a frescoed ceiling representing some scion of the eighteenth century nobility borne aloft by attendant Graces – many of whom were also burdened with his various armorials. This staircase gave us a private entrance to another street, which, though we were not supposed to know of it, enabled us to forestall the dawn without waking the night-porter. On one occasion, however, the key was lost, the porter to all intents and purposes drugged, and David was obliged to shout Simon and myself awake through a fourth floor window – to the surprise of the neighbouring inhabitants. It was only a vivid dream that he was being murdered in the gutter beneath by the Fascisti that induced me to go to the door and rush quite unnecessarily into the street in my pyjamas. We shared our staircase with the local branch of the Maritime Bank and a number of other residents, whom we used to frighten by prowling up and down it on tiptoe, until the cashiers began to think that they were the victims of a plot.

Next door but one was the Fascist Lodge, where meals were served to the members in an open courtyard. On the pavement of the arcade outside was inlaid the axe of the organization, surrounded by a wreath of laurel leaves. Thither we – or rather David and myself – had gone with our friend the night-watchman, to be enrolled; but it was unfortunately a necessary condition of membership that we should be permanent residents of Bologna. Though at times we began to think that this eventuality must be fulfilled, we never gave up hope of avoiding it. From our bedroom windows we could watch the activities of the local organization. One day three lorry loads of boys arrived back from a camping expedition. They seemed in high spirits. Fascismo is in fact a sort of boy scout regime; but instead of staves it carries revolvers. Italy is the victim not so much of a dictatorship, but of an ochlocracy, the rule of an armed mob, and an immature mob at that. Some slight account of the higher ideals of the party will be found in the last chapter but two.

The days passed in various ways. An up-to-date shop in the main square provided us with English books and papers. It also stocked the life of Henry Ford, translated into Italian. I read a number of the plays of Shaw. That a technique so completely inartistic, that these bare anatomical views of human nature, the bones of which are dried and classified, not always correctly, for the sole purpose of expressing the once rather shocking philosophy of the author, should have received such unanimous acclaim at the hands of the past generation, is an instructive commentary on the Edwardian struggle against Victorian hypocrisy. The antithesis, of course, is to be found in Chekov, whose edifices do not show their girders. For some reason, however, he is frequently described by the London Press as 'the Russian Shaw'. By the same process of thought we have always regarded El Greco as 'the Spanish Millais'.

As we sat about the cafés of the town we made various friends. I discovered Simon one afternoon talking unconcernedly in English to a man who could speak not a word of any language but Italian. He appeared to be a retired engine-driver living on twenty-five lire a day, who would be pleased to start work again if we could get him a job in England. Providence momentarily loosed my tongue to dilate on the prevalence of unemployment in that country, but I was cut short by his remarking that he knew some ladies whom he particularly wanted us to meet that evening. Simon also picked up with an Egyptian commercial traveller in cotton, who wore a red fez. He was much impressed by our acquaintanceship with a former ornament of Balliol College, Oxford, a countryman of his, whose brain after the Gordon legend, is said to be the greatest thing that Egypt has produced of late years. For Bologna, he seemed strangely ignorant of the whereabouts of the other sex. On the other hand, David, sitting by himself in a café, was suddenly joined by one of the Bersaglieri, who spoke a kind of *lingua franca*. At first they chatted, discussed barrack life and the origin of the cock's feathers that adorned his hat. He then announced that David must meet a certain lady – with her mother – whom he was entertaining tomorrow, Sunday evening. What the presence of the mother portended, David was unable to fathom.

One of the first things that we had noticed upon our arrival in the town was the quantity of posters on the hoardings displaying in large capitals the words

ALBA

V

BOLOGNA

Upon close inspection this legend, dated for Sunday, August 16th, resolved itself into an announcement for the Cup Final of all Italy. We ordered the hotel to procure us the best seats that were to be had, and were drinking vermouth prior to setting out for the field in the Via Toscana, when the engine-driver, whom we had re-encountered, hailed a friend of his. The friend was going to the match also. He refused a drink, but stood in a statuesque pose until we had finished ours. He then accompanied us. A party of four, we stepped into a taxi and joined the Derby Day crowd that was streaming out of the town to the scene of the match.

'Alba v. Bologna'. The affect of those three words upon the Latin temperament can scarcely be exaggerated. Imagine all the football crowds and Cup Final crowds that the world has ever seen; the queues outside the Ring; the downs at Epsom; the stands at Aintree. Multiply the checks, friz the hair, impressionize the neckwear and point the tan and chocolate brogues; accelerate the voices and the movements; cover the whole with a cloud of dust; and that will convey some impression of the voluble multitude with whom we pushed through the gates and into the stands. The field itself was small and, where there were no stands, surrounded by palings over which peeped tin advertisements and villa residences of red brick. For some reason it was marked out as for hockey.

The sun, now half-way down the heavens, seemed to suck away the little air that was left. Five o'clock arrived. The two teams ran sportingly on to the field at a gymnastic double, the captains of each bearing bouquets of tuberoses and pink carnations. The home team was champion of the north, and her captain had skippered Italy's international team last year. Alba was a Roman team, champion of the south. As the opposing sides lined up, the spectators became almost silent, so great was the tension. Then the ball was kicked off and the shouting began. We found ourselves seated in the midst of the Roman contingent, who were endeavouring, not unsuccessfully, to pit their lungs against the combined voices of Bologna's thousands. Later they began to take exception to the methods of the northerners, and a fight ensued two rows behind, which was stopped by the police.

The referee, a very plump man, received a good deal of abuse. But all minor excitements were drowned in the ear-splitting enthusiasm that greeted the first goal, shot by the Bologna captain after twenty minutes' hard play. His team fell about his neck and kissed him – an unpleasant spectacle in view of the physical conditions resulting from exertion in the extreme heat.

Half-time found the score 1–0 in Bologna's favour. Alba, at the beginning of the second half, showed more dash, and began

to press. In the last quarter of an hour, however, the side went
completely to pieces and eventually lost by five goals to none.
The players showed no ability to dribble, though at difficult
kicks, and at heading the ball, they were unusually apt. Any
attempt at a barge evoked volleys of protest, and was invariably
given as a foul. At every opportunity the crowd shouted 'OFF
SIDE!' and ''ANDS'. The winners, we were glad to think, had
been trained by an Englishman.

After it was over, it was utterly impossible to find a taxi.
The trams were invisible beneath the struggling humanity that
clung to their outsides like swarms of bees. And we had walked
half-way back before we found a cab. We returned to the
hotel and washed. Then we went to dine at a small restaurant,
embowered with oleanders, recommended by our companion,
who paid for the dinner. The conversation was in French.

Our new friend belonged to that familiar type who live
on their wits, and whose conversation, though containing a
sub-stratum of truth, is embellished with the fiction necessary
to their own glorification and the making of a good story.
His name was Alfredo Rossi, and he produced a visiting card
belonging to his brother, who was apparently a commercial
chemist engaged in the artificial manure trade. In appearance
he was thinly made and bony, standing about six foot one in
height. His lips were slightly pursed, the upper lip forming a
point in the middle, which rested on the lower. Sinister, staring
eyes moved inquisitively about beneath his hanging brows.
His face was dark, golden brown, and his hair was black.
His long body was clothed entirely in black; black shirt, black tie,
black handkerchief, black suit, and black buttoned boots. His
garments clung. In manner he was most friendly.

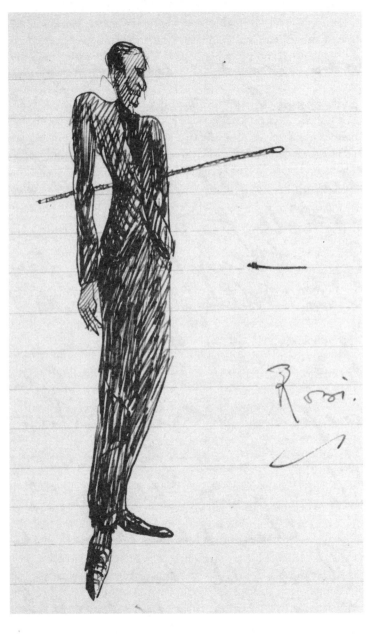

During the war he had fought on the Italian front and learned
to hate the French, having been at one time liaison officer where
one line ended and the other began. His particular company had
been dependent on the French commissariat and as a result had
almost starved. We were told later, that in Rome, after the war,
the waiters refused to serve French people in the restaurants,
so hated were they. This feeling has not disappeared.

On demobilisation, Rossi had joined d'Annunzio at Fiume.
Then, when that venture had been brought to its end, he had
become one of the first Fascisti, in the days when Fascisti were
openly murdered in the streets, and had fought, dislodged
and drowned in the moat the communists who had obtained
possession of the castle at Ferrara. He now represented
himself as Chief of the Ferrara Fascisti. Money flowed from
his pockets. He regretted, however, that he was unable to keep
a mistress as well as a wife. In the same breath he said that he
would show us round the town on the morning of the morrow;
and in the afternoon, if the car was still delaying us, would we
come out and see Ferrara with him, where he hinted vaguely
at a country house.

He arrived on Monday, as he said he would, at ten o'clock.
I was the only one dressed or even awake. His arm linked
in mine, we set out together, talking halting French. He
displayed the genuine love of good buildings and historical
association that is innate in nearly all Italians. First we visited
the old university. The walls were frescoed from wainscoat
to ceiling with the heraldic bearings of former professors
and distinguished students; amongst them were the names
of several Englishmen. Over a door was a bust of Cardinal
Mezzofanti, who received Metternich on one of his northern
Italian tours and spoke forty-two languages with fluency. We
were shown, also, the room fitted with carved stalls and a sort
of canopied throne at one end, in which human dissection
was first practised, with a papal inquisitor looking through a
hole in the wall, and Mass being celebrated underneath. Some
students, studying law, regarded us aghast. Napoleon, during

his short rule, had considered the old buildings inadequate and transformed them into a library, moving the seat of learning to others more capacious – an isolated example of the beneficial thoroughness which characterised his administrations. Thence we walked to a theatre, designed in the form of a horseshoe with splayed ends by Bibiena, and decorated in green and gold. This is one of the few eighteenth century theatres still intact. In general appearance, its balustradings are bolder and rather earlier than the delicate gold filigree work that covers the inside of the Fenice Theatre, at Venice. The morning finished with the picture gallery, containing a depressing collection of the less interesting *seicento* masters, and, as David remarked, more square feet of Guido Reni than all the rest of the world put together.

The chief objects of interest in the town are the magnificent fountain by Giovanni di Bologna – a native of Douai – supporting a triumphant Neptune attended by adoring nymphs; and the two towers, one unfinished, the other rising square and unadorned, to the height of 292¾ feet. This is known as the Torre degli Asinelli, having been built by a family of that name, and inclines 3 ft. 4 ins. from the perpendicular. Its neighbour is a dwarf, squat in appearance, being only 130 ft. high and slanting 8 ft. to the south and 3 to the east. The effect of these leaning piles, with scarcely twenty yards between the two, is most extraordinary. The only other tower that we saw that was at all comparable in slenderness and proportion to the higher of them was the machicolated dock tower at Grimsby, built at the entrance to the docks for hydraulic purposes. In this case the architect, perhaps unconsciously, has achieved a unique triumph in a country where the art of building single towers is practically unknown.

Diana, though promised, was not forthcoming that day. We set out that evening therefore in a hired car for Ferrara. The driver seemed unable to distinguish between the accelerator and the brake. It was dark, and the clouds of dust thrown up by the carts caught the light in confusing beams. The intervening country produced a disgusting stench that lay across the road in waves. On arrival at the sole hotel, we were ushered into the unconverted rooms of an ancient palace. On the walls were inlet canvas portraits of the former owners. Wooden-looking men and women cracked and torn and soured sneered aristocratically upon our slumbers from their settings of painted foliage and painted bas-reliefs.

We dined well, and drank a number of sticky native wines, tasting for the first time Malvasin or Malmsey. A liqueur named Grappé, distilled from the pips of grapes, completed the meal. Then we went for a walk and looked out over the city walls. At twelve o'clock we betook ourselves to bed, and Rossi departed to play poker. We were to take lunch with his family the following day at their country-place, and then go eel-fishing. For the present, goodnight.

The next morning he was gone. So, also, was David's snake-wood cane. Let us be charitable and suppose that his losses at poker compelled a retreat. Whatever his intentions, he made practically nothing out of us and spent a good deal. We were sorry to miss the eel-fishing.

Ferrara is a sleepy market town, lying in the midst of flat marshy country. The heat was such that by eleven o'clock the streets were deserted. It was here that Lucrezia Borgia, having at the age of twenty-five married Duke Alfonso d'Este as her third husband, reformed her character, spending 'the morning in prayer, and in the evening inviting the ladies of Ferrara to embroidery parties, at which accomplishment she was a great proficient'. The cathedral is twelfth century, with a triple-gabled façade vaguely reminiscent of Peterborough. Standing about it are a number of red marble lions. The interior is not interesting. A very beautiful building is the Palazzo dei Diamanti, so called from the diamond-cut restications with which the whole of the outside walls are ornamented.

But it is the castle, the old fortress of the d'Estes, that is the pride of the town, being the finest medieval fortress in Italy, and the finest brick building in the world. It is complete and untouched, never having been damaged or improved. Built entirely of brick, a great towering pile with several inner courts, it stands in the middle of the town surrounded by a broad walled moat. This is crossed on each side by drawbridges, that stretch from massive, square brick gate-houses, resting on spreading bases rising from the water, to tall projecting wings, heavily machicolated and corniced, that stand out a little way from the main building. The drawbridges are still in working order. The beauty of this massive fabric rising from, and reflecting down into, the cool, dark green waters of the moat, a delicate burnt pink against the vivid blue of the sky, is incomparable. The smallness, the perfect workmanship and preservation of the bricks, gives the whole a wonderful texture, the effect of which is completed by gleaming white stone copings and small white buttressed parapets that run round the tops of the towers. To the contemporary architect who favours the use of these small bricks and the maintenance of severe and simple lines, Ferrara Castle must constitute one of the greatest of the ancient masterpieces of architecture. It is the predecessor of such examples of twentieth century architecture as the new town hall at Stockholm, perhaps the finest of the world's modern buildings.

The disappearance of Rossi had, in a way, tended to raise our spirits. After lunch we hired a car and endured an insufferably hot drive back to Bologna, where we were thankful to sink into the comfort of the Baglioni. The car would really be ready tomorrow at midday.

That evening David and I, foreseeing the abysmal uncertainty of the morning, while waiting for Diana, determined to stay up all night, so that we should be able to sleep all day, until the car was actually at the door. With this end in view, we first visited a cinema. Italian films are usually exasperatingly short. This one, however, a series of glimpses from the life of Ivan the Terrible, was interminable. Italian historical producers understand dresses, but not settings. The long coats and tall fur head-dresses of the Boyars moved about against walls that might have decorated

Edwardian bathrooms. And the women were so virulently ugly, as to appear malformed. The atmosphere in the building thickened. The odour of patent-booted feet intensified. Above us, a wit, surrounded by a crowd of admiring 'chaps', found it necessary to Italianise each successive Russian name in that throaty voice that is the inevitable accompaniment of after-dinner audiences. In the vicinity lurked a baby. It was midnight before we had sat the performance out; and Simon was so exhausted that he went to bed.

David and I then went from café to café in search of the band that played latest. At length bandless, we sought a restaurant that was open from 4 am until 2 am, twenty-two hours out of the twenty-four. Here, homesick for the Lyons' all-night, we ordered bacon and eggs, which materialised into hard-boiled lumps of yellow and white bouncing about on sheets of raw ham. However, we ate them, and talked for a long time to the Fascist night-watchman who had joined us. At last, dropping with fatigue, we crawled up our private staircase and went to bed.

CHAPTER X

HAVING SUCCESSFULLY PASSED the whole morning asleep, we came down to a late lunch, to be told that the car would not after all be ready that day. This was the final straw, and with a great effort David lost his temper. He told the hotel what he thought of them and accused them of being in league with the garage. He repeated himself to the mechanics in German and French. He then made the hotel ring up the garage and telephone his feelings to the manager in Italian, adding that if the car was not forthcoming that evening, it would be removed without a farthing's payment for the week's work. That afternoon we spent in the workshop. And at tea-time, just as a slight shower of rain was beginning to disperse the heat, we were able to indulge a triumphant tour of the town in Diana's lap, proudly stopping before all the cafés where we had become known. We dined for the last time at our comfortable table in the corner, off newly-shot partridges, and left Bologna about eleven o'clock next morning, the combined staffs of the hotel and the garage bidding us goodbye and Godspeed, as we drove off with our pyramid of trunks and suitcases once more behind us. The sense of freedom as we mounted the outlying spurs of the Apennines and eventually became enveloped in wet masses of cloud, was ecstatic after the hot confinement of the arcades, and the company of disreputable Fascisti. The Lombardy plain behind us, we were now entering the hill country.

Since the Apennines run in a south-easterly direction and the Bologna-Florence road in a south-westerly, the curves and hairpin bends which the crossing of the mountains necessitated were more than usually alarming. The villages became plain and gloomy, with high, narrow streets of dull, grey, stone houses, the eaves of which began to project in the manner of all mountain dwellings. The cloud, which covered everything, was followed by a rainstorm, which left Simon in a rage and David huddled beneath an overcoat, from which only a nose and a pair of gloves protruded. Then, as we descended, the sun came out and the tiled and faceted egg of the *duomo* of Florence, rising from the distant white patches of town in the valley beneath, swung into view round a bend of hewn cliff. On the left, the white villas of Fiesole and the black points of their attendant cypresses spattered the irregular contours of a long purple brown face of hill. We passed the gilded gates of San Donato, the actual possession of which, like that of Arundel, confers a title, now borne by the family of Demidoff, who purchased it from the Pope. And eventually drew up outside the commanding gateposts, surmounted by lions, of the Villa Sassetti, the home of the Edens, whom we had come to see, and whose address we had suddenly remembered was in the Via Bolognese, down which we were freewheeling as fast as its surface would allow. The gates were shut. Through them, at the end of a long embanked avenue of cypresses that bridged an intervening valley like an aqueduct, the golden white face of the villa, with its green shutters, rose sedately from the surrounding vineyards against a background of Ilexes, and hill, and sky. I rang the bell; a motherly woman emerged from the lodge and looked suspiciously at us and our piles of luggage. She said that she would telephone to the house. Then she reappeared and asked me to come through a side-gate and telephone also. The lodge was full of sleeping forms. My efforts were of little use, as the footman at the other end could only speak Italian. But eventually the gates were opened, and we drove up the avenue, dirty and dishevelled, to the front door. The hall, through which we passed, was small and round and very high, being lighted by a skylight at the top; while below, a fountain was playing in a marble basin on a pedestal, at the bottom of which were goldfish drowsing on aquatic mosses.

The staircase was circular, and on a level with the landing at the top the wall was adorned with a series of frescoes by Tiepolo, lately removed from a palace in Venice, and slightly curved to fit their new position. We were greeted by Edward Eden, who came trotting down the stairs in a bottle-green suit, followed by his brother, Martin, in light grey. Martin is a poet. He writes finished verses, of intricate construction and polished rhythm. Just as the modern Hungarians have now begun to paint on what they call a 'cultural basis', relegating post-impressionism and its attendant realisms to a passing phase of anti-Victorian revolt – a revolt none the less Victorian for that – so the English writers, of whom Martin is one, are in process of discarding the fragmentary style of atmospheres and passing emotions that has characterized what is popularly termed 'modern poetry.' Martin has been termed a follower of the Sitwells. In reality, borne on the wings of a tireless vocabulary and an irresistible sense of verbal form, he has outstripped them. Both Edward and he seemed pleased to see us, finding August in Florence necessarily hot and dull.

We pottered round the terraced garden, admiring the baroque giants and dwarfs standing amid walls and niches of cut yew, fat stone plumes waving from their helmets and large armour-clad bellies hanging to their knees. Then we plucked and ate some yellow tomatoes, as big as grapefruit, imported from California. Returning to the house, we encountered Mr Eden, whom, despite his middle-age, has lately been the hero of all Florence, for having worsted in a duel a young Fascista who had picked a quarrel with him at a reception. They had fought with rapiers. He was most hospitable and begged us to 'take our meals at the villa'.

We drove down to Florence for tea, and in deference to David's passion for 'the best' took rooms overlooking the Arno at the Grand Hotel. Beneath sat a number of people fishing from the walled parapet of the roadway. The Arno is converted into a river by means of a municipal dam at one end of the town in order to give the various bridges with which it is spanned an air of sanity during the summer months. Beyond the dam was a large expanse of slime and shingle, upon which the youth of the town, shameless as God made them, were disporting themselves. Our rooms were exorbitantly expensive. We decided for once to have our money's worth. The hot water in the bath was not running as fast as might have been expected; within five minutes the plumbers had been summoned – and arrived. We then demanded two extra carpets; they were brought, and with them a writing table. The beds were moved and the mattresses changed. After that we contented ourselves with plucking shiny plaster fruits from the cheffonier and rearranging the scheme of a neighbouring Louis Quinze (Lancaster Gate period) boudoir, with the superfluous toilet ware from our bedrooms.

Having been separated from all news for three weeks, it was pleasant to receive our first letters, to learn that the family bulldog had unfortunately maimed a goat and that the bracken had, in places, grown to the height of nine feet. A firm of solicitors also wrote to demand the sum of six and sixpence owed to a client in bankruptcy; and an inhabitant of Wantage intimated that he would appreciate a recognition of his having picked up a box of my collars that had fallen out of the dickey of a two-seater seven weeks ago. He had ridden, he said, thirty miles one precious Saturday afternoon to return them. If I did not answer he threatened to expose me in the local press. I sent him a vulgar postcard.

Having changed, we drove up to dinner at the Villa, where we spent a delightful evening. Mrs Eden mixed us cocktails of her own invention. After dinner we went round the house. The bedrooms seemed to contain more of the collection than the rooms downstairs. Mr Eden had made several additions since I had been to lunch two years before. We ended up the evening, unforgivably late, on the roof of a grotto overlooking the lights of the town.

The next morning at 9.30 Martin and Edward arrived with unfailing punctuality, to take us out to see the sights. I alone went with them, and having visited the galleries and churches with great thoroughness on a previous visit, made no particular effort at formal sightseeing. There is nothing so pleasant as revisiting a town like ·Florence, when the monuments of the place are no longer weighing on the conscience. We wandered into the Bargello and stood before the Donatellos, the greatest portrait sculptures of European civilization; of which, beneath the rough-hewn corrugations which he mistakes for patine, Epstein is, of contemporary artists, the most direct follower.

We then visited the Palazzo Vecchio and wallowed in the titanic curves of Vasari's battlepieces. Here one can almost agree with Vasari's own opinion that he was the last of the great masters. A sixteenth-century map of England, frescoed on the wall of one of the apartments, was marked with the name of our local market-town, a place that has been of complete unimportance since the reign of John. After a fleeting glance at what Baedeker terms the 'vitreous paste of the Orsanmichele', we returned and as David and Simon were awake, went out and had lunch on the pavement of the Via Tornabuoni. The meal was prolonged by two cavernous flasks of *chianti*.

About three o'clock, having borrowed a cushion for the back seat, we set out to see the Certosa, a monastery on a hill outside the town, noted as the scene of the imprisonment of Pius VII by Napoleon. The rooms occupied by him are kept empty in sacred memory of the event, and adorned with badly-painted portraits of the martyr. The monastery, as a whole, possesses a beautiful atmosphere, aloof from the world, the embodiment of Tuscan peace and permanence. The sloping arcading, at the side of the broad shallow steps that lead up from the entrance gate, stood out creamy white against the hot pewter-blue of the sky. Oddly detached panoramas presented themselves through each successive arch: white villas perched on little hummocks; black points of cypresses, like the teeth of a broken comb; terraced rows of salad-green vines; and the ethereal grey of the round olives on their stunted trunks climbing the hills in dotted patches; all stood out against the inevitable range of solid mountains. A monk led us round; a fresco, half worn away, presented the same airy unreality as the olive leaves. In the middle of a spacious, cloistered courtyard, open to nothing but the turquoise imminence of the sky, stood a wellhead designed by Michael Angelo. Mounting the steps to it, the monk posed, white-robed and brown-bearded, and asked us to photograph him. The last visitors who had done so were from Copenhagen, and when they had reached home, they had sent him some snapshots of himself. We regretted that we had no camera. He, therefore, led us to what is apparently the *raison d'être* of the establishment. In a small room, furnished from floor to ceiling with shelves, there confronted us row upon row of bottles of every shape, substance and capacity, containing an unending variety of intoxicating liqueurs. Simon and Edward were unable to resist the guile of the reverend brother behind the counter. David purchased a large majolica flask to store away behind Diana's cushions in case of emergency. Martin, eyeing Edward disapprovingly, gulped down a miniature bottle holding rather less than a thimble; and I, who dislike liqueurs, asked for a glass of soda-water: at which, it is no exaggeration to say, the monk was genuinely shocked. Such was the lining of our Tuscan cloud.

After a further ten miles' driving, we came to Monte Gufoni, the home of the Sitwells, a fortified castle on a hummock. This low rambling collection of dilapidated courtyards and periods, surmounted by a medieval tower, is tenanted not only by that distinguished family, but a number of others, which they are unable to evict. The porter refused to let us enter the living-rooms with their Severini frescoes, despite all Martin's protestations of intimacy with the owners; but we were able to admire the shell and gold mosaic grotto and the terraced garden covered with flowers. The castle commands a magnificent view on all sides, but is so entirely surrounded by roads that any sense of privacy is lacking.

On our return, in the attempt to find the key to a palace that was shut, we drove round the town twice at high speed, each time inadvertently disregarding the upraised arms of the police. We arrived at the hotel and were leisurely dismounting, when a whole fleet of them, mounted on bicycles, arrived panting with rage and excitement and fined David a pound on the spot.

We then went to dinner at the Villa. Mrs Eden's cocktails, on top of the holy monk's liqueur, produced an explosive effect, and no sooner was the meal finished, than the whole party launched into a loud and acrimonious political discussion, in which Simon tried wildly to explain why the Birmingham group of the Labour Party, led by Oswald Mosley, must needs adopt the name of the most impregnable Conservative stronghold in the country. As people always regard Simon's advanced theories as either childish or unbalanced, he becomes not unnaturally annoyed. Mrs Eden and I laughed together in a corner.

The next day was Saturday. After finding that our bill was, for once, less than we expected, we drove off to Siena.

CHAPTER XI

ITALY IN AUGUST is not the quaint hippety-hop country of middle-aged water colourists that she appears in the Spring. The landscape of the Tuscan and Umbrian Apennines assumes a grim, forbidding aspect. The afternoon, as we set out for Florence, was thick and sultry, with thunder in the air. The sun had ceased to shine; it glowed through a molten haze; a sort of dull, yellow fog of heat overspread the whole land. Light and shade seemed to disappear.

We turned off the main road at Poggibonsi, having first entered the town and upset a hand-cart in our efforts to find a way out of it. A few miles up a side road brought us to San Gimignano, with her thirteen perfectly plain and haphazardly oblique fortified towers silhouetted against the skyline like a series of bowled wickets. At Easter time, two years ago, wallflowers were sprouting from the crevices of the towers, and the fruit trees were in bloom in the gardens. Now the place seemed deserted. We looked at the frescoes at Benozzo Gozzoli and drank some soda water, then drove out by the opposite gate along an ill-defined track, in the hope of coming to Volterra.

Gradually the country began to lose its vegetation. The hills developed longer and more sweeping curves; at the same time, as though convulsed by some uncontrollable agony, their sides were thrown into fissures and tumours of the most fantastic description. At the foot of each straggled a little grass, burnt a dirty brown, which, as though seared to dust beneath the furnace of the heavens, soon gave place to hot, grey powdery earth. Occasionally a couple of white oxen might be seen ploughing some precipitous slope, one of them standing two feet higher than the other, yet both harnessed to the same plough.

Volterra is situated on a rock, black and gloomy, looking out over long-drawn wastes of parched desolation. The site is of great age, Volterra having been the capital of the old kingdom of Etruria, and the last city to hold out against the Romans. She is now famed for her mines of alabaster, which is carved locally into battleships and motor-bicycles. As we zig-zagged up the face of the cliff, huge walls, remnants of the extinct Etruscan civilization, frowned their massive, uncemented blocks upon us.

We passed through the Porta dell'Arco, also Etruscan, a double gate thirty feet deep. At this point a small boy hopped on to the car, and we drove about the town under his direction, to the envy of his fellows.

We eventually came to a stop between the baptistery and the cathedral. This latter supports a dome designed, like that of the *duomo* at Florence, by Brunelleschi. As if to add to the sinister atmosphere of the place, the ancient fortress has been converted into a convict prison. Also, owing to a slow subsidence of their foundations, the majority of the churches are beginning to fall over the cliff. Our urchin informed us that he was one of the few certified guides in Volterra. When, after a long absence in the cathedral, I thought it advisable to make sure that no one was molesting the car, he remarked in a tone of offended indignation: 'There are thieves in Florence, in Rome, in Milan; in Volterra, only gentlemen.'

It was dark by the time we reached Siena.

Siena reigns supreme among the hill towns. The architecturally fastidious may affect to dislike her black and white cathedral, with its Neapolitan wedding cake façade, that dominates the town like a great, humped zebra sitting on a rock. These same purists will, however, be lost in admiration of the primitives with which the Palazzo Publico is frescoed, many of which, especially the panoramic battlepieces, are unlike any to be found elsewhere. They are done in much the same style as those decorative memorials of the battle of Tel-el-Kebir and the triumphs of Sir Garnet Wolseley in the Soudan, which still adorn the walls of old-fashioned public houses. Most attractive of all is the equestrian portrait, executed in 1328 by Simone Martini, of Guidòriccio da Folignano di Reggio attending the siege of Montemassi, a painting mentioned above as the nearest analogy – in two dimensions – to the statue of Can Grande at Verona. High up on the end wall of a large room there rides a solitary man upon a horse, in the midst of an oblong, dark blue landscape, relieved by fortresses, palisades, tents and attendant armies drawn and shaded in opaque, yellowish grey. The man himself is puffed with satisfaction, and the horse, prancing along beneath him, is draped from top to bottom in a yellow robe adorned with diagonal black lozenges.

In a neighbouring room is a series of life-size representations of the triumph and eventual funeral of Victor Emmanuel II, first king of Italy, one of whose many coats reposes in a glass case beneath. The sleek realism with which these illustrations of Italy's unification have been depicted by the artist is enhanced by the fact that he has so contrived his compositions, that the brilliant patches of red upon the uniforms, the green grass, and the great airy spaces of white sky, convey without a moment's hesitation an impression of the Italian national flag. The art to which the exploits of Garibaldi, Cavour, Mazzini, and the House of Savoy gave birth in the seventies and eighties still awaits recognition as one of the most widespread, if not meritorious, intellectual phenomena of the nineteenth century. There is not a town or a villa throughout the length and breadth of Italy where it is not represented. Here indeed is a novel and fruitful subject to which the ever-increasing body of artistic commentators may turn their attention. The style culminates in the frescoes in the Vatican, perpetuating the proclamation of the Infallibility of the Pope, in which the Holy Father is represented standing firmly on the red baize steps of his throne, while a ray from Heaven strikes his uplifted visage in the presence of an applauding crowd.

The great beauty of Siena is the main piazza, fashioned like one of those fan-shaped shells that are found on the sands, with the ribs marked out in stone. At its foot, adjoining the Palazzo Publico, rises the Mangia, a very tall, slender, brick tower, stone-machicolated, and supporting on its topmost platform a bell, beneath the gaping metal mouth of which it is possible to stand and survey the view. As though from an aeroplane, the whole of Tuscany stretches away on every side. In the foreground on its altar of rock, stands the cathedral, with its black ringed campanile, and its dome, a delicate white shell, now visible. Diverging from it lies the town, hemmed in by the encasing walls, with the streets lined in black shadow against the sunbaked brilliance of the rough tiled roofs.

It was at Siena, in the Spring of 1923, that we arrived to find the whole town *en fête*, the windows hung with arras – whatever arras is – and the entire population lining the narrow streets and converging on to the open space beneath the façade of the cathedral. As we watched, amid intense, yet restrained excitement, there materialised, ensconsed in a pre-war taxi, the embalmed hand of St Francis Xavier. The whole multitude fell on its knees to the ground as the vehicle approached. Seated bolt upright on the worn, black leather seat, a bishop in mitre and cope, inclined the shrivelled relic and its emerald ring from side to side, blessing the crowd. The arrival was followed by an impressive ceremony in the cathedral, so largely attended that little boys were to be seen seated among the large altar candlesticks. As a result the floor was boarded up to prevent it from damage. This year, however, it was uncovered and we could admire the superb drawing of the incised battle-pictures, with which it is emblazoned.

The ten frescoes, ordered by Pope Pius III to commemorate the papacy of his uncle, Pius II, with which the Piccolomini library leading from the cathedral is adorned, are too well known as the consummate achievement of Pinturicchio, to justify superfluous comment; the magnificence and freshness of their colour has lost nothing during four hundred years.

Equally familiar is the pulpit of Niccolo Pisano, with its groups of supporting pillars resting on the backs of lions marchant. A curious and less noticed feature of the building is the frieze of the heads of all the Popes, running on either side of the main aisle above the Gothic arches, among which, as Elizabeth Barrett Browning has remarked:

... ... Joan
And Borgia 'mid their fellows, you may greet,
A harlot and a devil.

Much has been written of this building and the works of art beneath its roof. More no doubt is to come. But there is one sentence which expresses to perfection that particular genius, a mixture of extreme splendour and mysterious solemnity, that characterizes the cathedral; a sentence which describes it as the supreme example of what 'the unassisted genius of the Italians' could produce 'when influenced by medieval ideas'. In this rare combination lies the whole secret of the spiritual magnificence of early Italian art.

The day after our arrival was a Sunday and the streets of the town were paraded by bands representative of the various *contradi* in their medieval dresses of tights, doublets, and feathered 'Caps of Maintenance', who attracted attention by banners and drums. This curious survival of the parochial rivalries of the Middle Ages reaches its climax in the Palia, a racing fixture held twice yearly in the piazza, in which each *contrada* is represented by one or two riders, while the majority stand in the middle and beat one another with staves. In the afternoon we went to present a letter of introduction to Donna Issa Chigi at the Palazzo Chigi, a large building, the ground floor of which was converted into shops. She was away in the country, about two miles outside the town. We did not feel capable of following her.

The next day we set out in the afternoon for a motor drive. The heat was suffocating, and the sun was still invisible behind the lowering haze, which seemed to have become intensified. The land was the colour of burning pewter, patched with deadened ochres. Now and then the green streaks of a vineyard or the effervescent grey of an olive grove would take shape on the side of an approaching hill. Our objective was Pienza. It was here that the famous scholar and agnostic, Aeneas Sylvius, Pius II, built himself a palace, and, in fact, created the whole town, which remains exactly as when it came into being by his command five hundred years ago. The palace is built round three sides of a court, the fourth of which is left open to a wonderful view and is still inhabited by the Piccolomini, of which family Pius II was a member. A contemporary fresco-portrait still looks from over the door of his bedroom at the golden-pillared bed in which he slept. The rooms are small, and surmounted by fifteenth-century ceilings that have preserved their original decorations, consisting of a large number of painted beams crossing and re-crossing. The wallpapers, more modern, are reminiscent of William Morris. One room was occupied by a delightful miniature theatre in the Greek style, painted white and gold, with a tiny gallery at the back.

Later, we continued to Montepulciano, a hill town in a state of dilapidation. The once imposing tomb of Bartelomeo Aragazzi, by Donatello, has been split up all over the cathedral. One of the friezes, now part of the altar, consists of cupids and wreaths in soft relief. Its fellow is in the National Gallery. The town hall has a tower which I insisted on ascending in order to view Lake Trasimene, which could not be seen for the increasing haze. The others sat below.

On the way home I began to develop a headache. We had not gone far before the silencer fell off, and David and I were obliged to lie full length on our backs, in three inches of stifling dust and filth, and tie it on again with our handkerchiefs. As it was red-hot, this was not easy.

Late that night, the storm which had been threatening for so long broke on the hills with a terrific vehemence. After emptying the heavens of water, it began to blow with such force that the tiles rained off the roofs like dead leaves. The noise resembled a cinema orchestra accompanying a battle film. The orange trees in the courtyard fell against each other like a pile of drunken women; and Simon's little octagonal boudoir (Gothic 1820) was deluged with flying earth, which landed in clouds on his bed and befouled the clean linen in his open trunk.

Next morning the air was cool and fresh. We lunched at Arezzo, where we were held up twenty minutes at a level crossing. In the afternoon we passed along the shores of Lake Trasimene, but any desire to bathe was dispelled by a soaking downpour of rain that had wetted us to the skin before we had time to put up the hood. During the delay we were able to pluck large bunches of black grapes, which we ate as we drove along. We arrived at Perugia for dinner.

CHAPTER XII

PERUGIA IS THE STOCK HILL TOWN. It is not as picturesque as most and has manufacturing suburbs, which produce chocolate and pencils. But in the middle of the last century there arrived upon the scene the celebrated M. Brufani, who proceeded to plant on top of the cliffs an English family hotel. This he adorned with portraits of Queen Victoria, Edward, Prince of Wales, and Mr Gladstone, and thus made famous and popular the least interesting of Tuscan and Umbrian cities. The earliest known painting of Raphael, the largest stained-glass window in the world, and a series of moon-faced and boneless frescoes in the Sala del Cambio by Perugino, whose figures always have an air of being 'stuffed and done to a turn', are the chief objects of interest .

The electric light of the city is of a dubious quality. In my experience it has gone out twice and left my whole hotel to the mercy of a box of nightlights. While only a year previously the grandmother of a friend of ours had been carried fainting to the roof of a building by an uncontrollable lift, where she remained for an hour and a half, having only a few months before been precipitated from the top to the bottom of one of London's largest stores in another. Finally, even during the short eighteen hours of this present visit, our evening café was plunged into darkness for twenty minutes; and by the time that the lights had gone on again, the band had retired in despair.

As a tourist centre, this town seems to exercise an irresistible attraction for Americans. The visitors at Brufani's, under the influence of a 'family hotel', were disarmingly chatty. I was writing some letters one morning before breakfast, when a voice from out of an elaborately coiffured head, surmounted by a toque of pheasants' breasts, broke on my peace with the words: 'Say, young man, you look about the right age to inform me whether it was right here in Perugia that Shakespeare staged "The Taming of the Shrew".'

And again, just as we were hurrying out one evening to an appointment for which we were already late, we were buttonholed in a swing-door by an animated professor, who was anxious to inform us that he had been given a year's holiday, with travelling expenses paid, to go wherever he liked, and that though only four months of it were over, he wished he was nowhere so much as 'back over in Chicago, setting down to a good meal of buckwheat fritters and clams'. We seconded his desire.

Fifteen miles away, clinging scab-like to the mountainside, is Assisi, also monopolized by the English-speaking peoples. There are at least to be seen here, however, the finest of Giotto's frescoes, especially that of St Francis calling water from the rock, the companion to the famous picture of his preaching to the birds. For the rest, there is something disillusioning in struggling round a grated cloister in the company of a battalion of well-meaning but loud-voiced matrons and their daughters, to view the plantation of those emasculated bushes into which St Francis is supposed to have fallen, and eventually carrying away a little sprig of thornless rose-leaves encased in an illuminated sachet, for which five lire have been paid. One cannot help feeling that the money taken would be better devoted to the provision of soap for the monks, rather than the relief of a fictitious poor.

We did nothing in Perugia. David, to annoy, pretended that he liked the place and wished to see its sights. Simon and I, by subterfuges, prevented anything of the sort, and next morning insisted on starting at once. The drive was most confusing. We accidentally left the town on the Assisi road, and had to go right up the hill and into it again before finding our way out on the right side. Then, after about ten miles, we lost the main road in the mountains. Every turning that we took ended, after leading us five miles along it, in a village perched on some impregnable promontory of rock. Then down a street no wider than herself, Diana, amid a crowd of gesticulating men, women and children, bleating goats, braying asses, patient oxen and fluttered fowls, would back slowly out again, turn round, and after an operatic converse with the population, retrace her tracks and endeavour to take the second turning after the two pine trees by the white house, as instructed. At length, however, we found a continuous mountain path, which pursued its way up the steepest peaks and down the most bottomless valleys with irresistible pertinacity. For some twenty miles we crept along this ledge, corkscrewing up between woods of stunted oaks with fresh, light-green leaves, until on the top of the range, we finally rejoined the telegraph wires.

Round the next corner, Orvieto came in sight. In the foreground of an enormous landscape, dominated in one distant corner of the horizon by the dome of Monte Fiascone, there reared the rocky shape of some gigantic Stilton cheese, with Orvieto spread over the top and the white Gothic spikes of her cathedral peaking querulously above a sea of roofs. The sky was overcast with low black clouds and the city on her platform stood out a mysterious dark blue from a panorama outlined in the delicate tints of smoke arising from a bonfire of dead leaves. We descended by a series of twenty-five hairpin bends into this tremendous valley and then curveted our way up the road cut in the cliff beneath the town, in time for a late lunch at the hotel. A gramophone from behind two glass folding-doors was playing some dance tunes of three years ago.

From the hotel we walked to the cathedral, which is not unlike that of Siena, save that the black and white stripes are carried out in stone instead of marble, and thereby lose much of their effectiveness. The three main doorways alternate with four large panels of primitive bas-reliefs illustrating the Creation and other Bible incidents. The doors themselves are flanked by twisted columns of marvellous intricacy and elaboration, ornamented with Cosmati-work, a sort of gold and coloured inlay, that winds in and out of their circuitous flutings.

The interior is famous for the frescoes of Signorelli, which are said to have inspired those by Michael Angelo in the Sistine Chapel. In revolt from Perugino and his school, which included Raphael, Signorelli was the first artist to study anatomy; and his pupil, Michael Angelo, profited by his example. It was he, Signorelli, who first made his figures stand upon the ground. They grip the earth with a kind of prehensile intensity that tautens the muscles of their calves like knotted rope and leaves those of the spectator aching in sheer sympathy.

From Orvieto we motored to Viterbo, and without entering the town went straight to the Villa Lante to see the gardens, designed in their entirety by Giovanni di Bologna. The Italian garden, if not one of the greatest contributions made by that country to civilization, is one of the most purely pleasurable. That of the Villa Lante is small and not so obviously magnificent or such a feat of engineering as the fountains and cascaded terraces of the Villa d'Este at Tivoli. The whole design is subordinated to the course of a single stream, which flows down from a wooded hill behind. Even the house is divided into two square blocks in order to preserve the effect of symmetry. Right at the back, where the woods begin, the stream falls wildly over a small declivity of fern-grown rock, to find itself confined in a dark, still pool, heavily shaded beneath the myriad leaves of ancient, twisted ilexes. On either side stand the cracked and pillared façades of two old moss-grown pavilions. The stream then descends from terrace to terrace in a series of sloping troughs about twenty feet long and eighteen inches wide. The first of these is square and massive like an elongated sarcophagus with a broad brim curving slightly downwards at the edges. The second is shallow, and shaped in a succession of formalized scallop shells, not only at the sides but on the bottom, so that the water itself is cast into a regular design as it ripples down the moulded surface to the next terrace.

The stream is then received in a semi-circular basin, ruled by two recumbent Tritons, barely distinguishable beneath their coating of ferns and moss. From the balustrading above them expectorating lions assist the downward course of the waters. Between the two blocks of the villa they flow and come to rest in a large open square, laid out like a Dutch garden: but in place of beds is water, and in place of box hedges, stone. The climax is reached in the bronze group of four male figures upholding the Lante crest, a pile of mountains surmounted by a star, from the innumerable points of which, at all angles and from all planes, long thin jets of water rise into the air like the tail of a spun-glass bird, and form a rainbow against the sun. This square, the only part of the garden that is not heavily shaded by ilexes, is separated from the attendant town by a high, grey stone wall. In the middle of this, in line with the course of the water and the troughs, is an archway, through which can be discerned the main street, sloping downhill to an indistinct vista of mountains on a distant horizon. Being the summer, the Duke of Lante was in residence, and we were not allowed, as formerly, to examine the lower part of the garden.

Driving back to the town, itself famous for its ancient fountains, we went to the papal palace, a ruin with a beautiful raised loggia, Gothic arcaded, supported on the side of a hill by one huge pillar. Through the tracery could be discerned a view of a domed church, standing out on the other side of a valley against a sky already pink with evening light. It was here that the two-year election of Martin V, who started the schism and went to Avignon, took place. Public opinion was so incensed at the delay that the building was de-roofed and the cardinals left to debate in the rain. Hence the ruin. Simon was full of historical theories about it. Viterbo is a curious decayed town, very old in appearance, with twelfth-century balconies and staircases still clinging to the outside of the houses. We left at about six o'clock on the last stage of our journey to the Eternal City.

Simon had expressed a desire to see the dome of St Peter's from afar, rising as it does, like some huge mauve bulb out of the landscape. The road turns a corner and far below in the plain it suddenly appears. This is the view, this first glimpse of Rome amid her halo of the past, that has thrilled so many statesmen, writers, artists and pilgrims to ecstasy, the culminating moment in the 'Grand Tour' of other days. Late as it was, we still had hopes that despite the fifty miles, we should catch sight of the cupola before dark.

The absurd ups and downs of the northern Apennines were now finally behind us, and the country assumed a lonely and uninhabited aspect. The hills rose and fell in wild, sweeping curves; a vast plain appeared, edged with mountains in the very far distance; out of the foreground rose Soracte, like the shadowy crest of a wave arrested in mid-air; on the right, deep in the purple shadows of a great hollow, a lake glistened like a mirror of burnished silver, as the setting sun slanted its rays over the unrippled surface of the water. The road had been mended since David and I had traversed it in 1924 and 1923, and we looked eagerly for the corner round which St Peter's should appear.

But it was not to be. At a small town named Roncigliano, climbing down the side of a steep cobbled street, a dense crowd barred our way: well-to-do shop-keepers; peasants come in from the country, the holsters of their arm-chair saddles bristling with bottles; and the inevitable brass bands in uniform. We waited half-an-hour expectantly, amused rather than annoyed at the delay. Suddenly, with no preliminary warning, there was a clatter, a roar from the crowd, and two men in faded jockey's colours rode full gallop up the cobbles on two small, stockily-built chestnut horses. This, however, was only a preliminary heat. The winner was led to one side and covered by a horse-rug embroidered with a large coronet. We hurried on before it could happen again.

We had not gone ten miles further when Diana, emitting a series of agonised coughs, stopped dead in her tracks. With sickening apprehension for the magneto, we leapt out, to discover that she had run out of petrol. We filled the tank, but still she refused to move. It was now almost dark and the road was deserted. With great resolution, Simon and I stopped the first car that came along. In the back sat a fat man in a straw hat and bow tie, accompanied by an extremely fat woman in a pink muslin *decolleté*, against whose swarthy skin Roman pearl earrings and a Roman pearl necklace glistened in that peculiarly rotund manner in which Roman pearls glisten against swarthy skin. The man spoke English. He requested me to sit in front by the chauffeur. The car was a cheap little Fiat limousine, upholstered in fancy embroideries and sporting a spray of artificial grass from a silvered icecream horn.

We had not gone four miles before David caught us up. Diana was restored, having been pushed to the top of the nearest hill. She had refused to move owing to an air-lock, caused by David's having accelerated on an empty tank. With effusive thanks and many apologies, I changed cars once more. Immediately afterwards we had a puncture; and it was nine o'clock before we arrived outside the Hotel de Russie, just off the Piazza del Popolo. We dined in the garden amidst electric fairy lights buried in beds of begonias, and dangling like fruit in a protestant Heaven from two poplars and a giant acacia. After a walk up the Corso, we went to bed.

CHAPTER XIII

THE CHARM OF ROME is a hackneyed subject; but one aspect of it that writers usually fail to mention is the colour with which so many of the buildings are coated. It is difficult to describe this particular shade. The effect is as though a kind of dull burnt orange had been covered with a roseate wash, yet at the same time the whole is flat and restful. Our rooms at the Russie – a hotel which the others affected to dislike as I had recommended it – gave out on to a large, leaded expanse of roof, surrounded on three sides by walls of this colour, against which the now flowerless wistaria climbed in festoons of green. Towards sunset the tints became intensified to an extent that one would have believed impossible outside the limelight of Drury Lane. The Fascisti, impelled by a secret hankering after skyscrapers and municipal Gothic, hold that this colour is incompatible with the dignity of a great capital, and have given orders that it shall be used no more. It is only natural that they should prefer that Italy should live in the present rather than the past. But there is something a little grotesque about the hysterical modernity that has inspired such edicts as this, and the threatened prohibition of the gondolas in Venice.

Letters were waiting for us at Cook's and at the Embassy. In one of his, David was bidden by a friend to pay a visit to an attaché at the Vatican Legation, named Harold Mott. Fetching Diana from her garage, we set off in search of him. After some difficulty, we unearthed the Vatican Legation from beneath a heap of debris, half-way up a ruined house, apparently in process of demolition. The attaché, we were informed through a grating, lived in an appartment in the Palazzo Doria, at the far end of the Corso. To the Palazzo Doria we went, and after climbing several long and exhausting flights of shallow stairs, were ushered, not into the expected attic, but into a large suite of rooms, parquet-floored and beautifully furnished, one as big as a London ballroom, the others equally spacious, though not so long. Mr Mott, in London trousers affixed to his waist by a brown leather belt, seemed surprised at the apparition of two young men disturbing his quiet afternoon. He gave us tea and was most hospitable.

That evening we stepped into a taxi, purposing to dine at a certain restaurant known to David. It proved to be shut. We were wondering what to do, when the driver took the bit between his teeth and motored us a long way out into the country to a restaurant overlooking the city. The main feature of the view was the red, white and green electric sign presented to Rome by Italian colonists in South America as a token of their affection. The taxi waited while we had our meal, then drove us back to a cabaret at the Apollo in the Via Nazionale. The last item on the programme was an *apache* dance, rendered with all the fire and passion of the Paris underworld. 'La Tigresse', spurned by the man she loves, plunges a knife into his back; the grip upon her throat gradually relaxes; she stands immobile, staring; then falls, a crumpled heap, by the side of him whom she has murdered; and remains, her frame shaken only by convulsive, racking sobs, as the music draws to a close. Curtain. Five minutes later a plump little woman on the wrong side of thirty-five, painted, and wearing a black neckband, trots up to our table and seats herself, with the words:

'*Moi, j'étais "la Tigresse".*'

Upon enquiry she proved to be a German, and, after our first surprise at her arrival, entertained us for the rest of the evening.

At a neighbouring table a loose-knit student of the University College Hospital was having the time of his life. He said his name was Walker. We stayed until late watching his gyrations. On our way home, the sporting spirit, latent in all Englishmen, bubbled to the surface with what might have proved disastrous results. We decided to run a race down the tunnel beneath the Quirinal. As the white-tiled roof echoes every sound a thousandfold, we made perhaps more noise than we realised in the utter silence of the early morning. I was slightly ahead, when suddenly, by some inexplicable means, a cordon of fifteen police appeared across the middle of the road. With an adroit swerve I negotiated these, to be confronted thirty yards in front by a second line. Not having enough breath to continue, I surrendered quietly. The others, who had not realised what had happened, were astonished at suddenly finding themselves arrested by thirty policemen. Simon produced his card. We walked off to the police station, guarded as though a rescue was expected.

The police station, or rather the room in which we were imprisoned, contained three iron beds covered with coarse brown blankets. On two of these reposed men who had not shaved for several days. We tried to talk to one of them, who resented it. The heat was stifling, so that it made us uncomfortable even to move. We talked to one another, then fell asleep. Eventually, after about two hours, a man with several chins arrived and said in a surly voice that as we were English people we might go. David said that if that was the reason we would not go, and demanded an explanation. None was forthcoming, so we did go.

The hotel contained several families of Americans who spent their day in the lounge because it was too hot to go out, while at night they danced with embarrassing vigour on a marble floor to a jazz band that possessed a number of ambitious instruments but no syncopation. Simon, who boasts that he can always pick an acquaintance with anyone in an hotel, picked one with them by winning eighty lire off the gambling machine in the bar and thus attracting their attention. The only good that came of it was that they introduced us to a little man named Petruccicroce, who took us to dine at a restaurant in the slums, where we could none of us eat the pudding that he had ordered. He worked on the Bourse, and was very proud of

his Oxford trousers, made in Rome. His clothes, as imitation
English, were satisfactory with the exception of his hat. With
him we visited other cabarets. But Roman night life was not
entertaining at this time of the year, the Bonbonnière, where
everyone habitually goes, being shut.

During our stay, in fact, we did very little. I spent a whole
day in bed, until my inside was settled by some Italian pills.
We dined one evening in the Borghese Gardens; and we
lunched at the Ulpia, a dark disused basilica, accoutred in the
Roman 'warming-pan' style – the lamps and hat racks being
constructed of hammered iron, into the midst of which, where
possible, had been introduced modern reproductions of coarse
classical pottery. Most of our time was occupied with visits to
and from Cook's, who were making arrangements for shipping
the car from Brindisi. They were not obliging.

David and I did succeed one morning in paying a visit to
St Peter's. The late summer sun cast a liquid golden brown
light over the sweeping colonnades and their double rows of
massive pillars, that contrasted strongly with the staring blue
of the sky. Dwarfed beneath the glittering white pyramids of
water shot up by the two central fountains, black crowds
of Holy Year pilgrims crawled ant-like across the piazza.
The stone of Rome is never grey; be it on wall or pavement,
it seems somehow to reflect, however faintly, that dull burnt
orange, with its flat pink glow.

Now that baroque art is fashionable and Ruskin cast into
the pit, it is to be hoped that the obedient public will soon
be treated to a book on the monuments of St Peter's. Why
comb the crevices of Apulia and the slums of Naples for gems
of architectural ornament, when here popes with black faces
and golden crowns are wallowing twice life-size in the titanic
folds of marble tablecloths, their ormolu fringes festooning
upon the arms of graceful skeletons, to disclose some Alice-
in-Wonderland door or the grim hinges of some sepulchral
grill? Those who have given rebirth to the ceilings of Tiepolo
and Solimena remain oblivious of their molten and chiselled

counterparts reposing in the more obvious environment of the largest church in Christendom. The Romans were vulgar before the rest of Europe had even become refined.

Apart from such individual masterpieces as the above, the interior of St Peter's as an artistic achievement is not impressive. Nor in all its details can the outside be termed faultless. There can seldom have lived a good artist with such capacity for bad art as Bernini. Able, as a sculptor, to produce work of such beauty as the group of Apollo and Daphne in the Villa Borghese, or the bust of William Baker in the South Kensington Museum, he has at the same time descended to posterity as the author of those grotesque apostolic giants that heave their uneasy draperies around the feet of the pillars beneath the dome of St Peter's. And while, as an architect, he could conceive the magnificent curves of the flanking colonnades, his also is the responsibility for the mean, unconvincing façade, with its ugly row of top-heavy biblical statuary. The result is that at the mention of the Classical style in ecclesiastical architecture there is no unchallenged masterpiece that immediately springs to the mind, as the names of Chârtres or Beauvais inevitably materialize at the suggestion of the Gothic. London has St Paul's, Vienna the Karlskirche, Paris the Madeleine, Berlin 'the Cathedral'; yet these are individual rather than international monuments.

But there exists, nevertheless, one cathedral in Europe which has never received recognition at the hands of any reputable section of artistic opinion – a recognition which it deserves, not only for its own intrinsic beauty, but as the foremost extant example of one of the most dignified and harmonious of post-Renaissance styles – that which is generally known as 'Regency', or, more accurately, 'Greek Revival'. This is the cathedral of Esztergom, in Hungary, the foundation stone of which was laid in 1822. In character it can best be compared to the front of the Haymarket Theatre, in London; in size and approximate plan, to St Paul's. As an instance in stone of style that is, unfortunately, almost invariably found in stucco, it is unique.

Those who have made the journey from Vienna to Budapest upon a Danube steamer will recall the towering outline of this massive temple, dwarfing the straggling town of Esztergom from its eminence of rock and dominating for miles around the flat landscapes of Hungary and Czechoslovakia between which swirls the immense stream of opaque, grey water. It was upon this rock that '*der heilige Stefan*', first king of Hungary, had his chapel, which to this day can be identified from the streets below by two little windows cut out of the cliff beneath the foundations of the main building. At the beginning of the nineteenth century, when the nationalism of Hungary, which was to erupt twenty years later, under Kossuth, was already in process of fomentation, it was decided to construct a cathedral that should surpass in the splendour of its dimensions any which Vienna, or indeed the whole Austrian Empire, could boast. The cusps and crockets of the Gothic Revival had not yet vanquished that regrettably short-lived fashion for simplicity that had lately revolted from the threadbare forms of the Romano-Italian in favour of the severe lines and sparse ornament of the Greek. And a design was chosen, which, but for an elaborate approach of· fountains and avenues, was carried out and consecrated within the space of four years. Thus completed, unlike so many cathedrals, according to the original plan, the church of Esztergom stands alone as the finest single edifice of early nineteenth century architecture in existence.

Viewed from the front, the plan is simple. In the centre there rises from a flight of steps that stretch the whole length of the middle block a vast pediment as high and as broad as the whole body of the church, supported on eight massive Corinthian pillars. Directly above this, though in fact set back upon the further portion of the building, is the dome, a slightly abbreviated semi-circle, resting on a heavy round and plain double cornice, which, in its turn, is supported by a ring of twenty-four Corinthian pillars set slightly away from the inner shell. To either side, flush with the inner doorways and behind the portico, rise tall square blocks with faceted corners, which are surmounted by round towers of the same diameter and half the height, also roofed with miniature flattish domes. The masonry joining these flanking towers to the main block is pierced by arches about forty feet in height, though comparatively small. Above each of these are inlet oblong bas-reliefs, which, with inconspicuous round plaques on either of the flanking towers, constitute the only external ornament. The stone is still light and in perfect preservation.

On entering, the visitor is confronted by a large oblong bas-relief of bronze, set in a background of dull red marble. The main body of the church is, like St Peter's, lined with grey marble, finished with flat Corinthian pilasters gilded at the capitals. Above the side altars are inlet large sheets of what appears to be lapis lazuli, with falling garlands of gold in classical designs upon them. The dome is gold and white, and below it are four saints on gold mosaic backgrounds. The stupendous empty expanse of floor beneath, which stretches into the transepts containing the side altars, is tessellated in a radiating design of black and white marble. Over the high altar is the largest altar-piece in the world, painted by Grigoletti; though inoffensive, it embodies the worst characteristics of the Guercino tradition. The chancel is raised.

The treasury contains the coronation copes and mitres of Hungary, and a number of glittering jewelled relics. The Dean, when he learnt that we were Protestants, could scarcely be persuaded to show us round, but was reconciled when we assured him that we were in no way allied with the German Evangelicals, who, in his opinion 'had no religion'; and that the bishops of the English Church carried crooks. After signing our names in the vestry and receiving his blessing, we returned to our hotel to lunch, where, as the Dean himself had been candid enough to suggest, we suffered considerably from fleas. This was in 1924.

CHAPTER XIV

WE SET OUT FROM ROME at one o'clock on Sunday afternoon, leaving the town by the Lateran Gate and the Appian Way. Aqueducts fretted the horizon, and tombs of forgotten emperors sprouted from the vineyards as we drove along the fringe of the Campagna. A brown tram runs by the side of the road, connecting the capital with Frascati and the Alban Hills. We had not gone fifteen miles before the near hind tyre collapsed with a loud report. The driver of a tram, which was labouring up the slight incline on which we had stopped, drew up beside us, and the passengers leant their heads out of the windows and crowed with pleasure, as they watched us raising Diana's very heavy load upon an extremely inadequate jack. The road was bad, but improved when it ceased to be the Appian Way. It became unswervingly straight and quite flat for thirty miles, along the side of a completely straight canal and beneath a completely straight range of mountains. The utter straightness of everything began to affect our nerves. We became giddy with rectitude. David could hardly hold the road. At last we came in sight of the sea. This was the first glimpse that we had had of it since we had turned our backs on the stagnant waters of the Hamburg docks.

On a rocky white promontory, jutting out into the dazzling ultramarine of the Mediterranean, stood the town of Gaeta, where Maria of Bavaria had made her last heroic stand for the Neapolitan Bourbons in 1860, holding the town for four months against the Sardinian fleet. As we watched, another tyre slowly flattened. A hundred yards further on we were obliged to wait at a level crossing, where two *Wandervögel*, caked with dust and sweat, gazed beseechingly at us. As we were now without a spare wheel, David, who is a great believer in the good luck that follows charity, offered them a lift. We did not have another puncture.

Diana now presented an extraordinary appearance, as though of some group of ornamental statuary moving along the southern Italian roads – to the bewilderment of their more regular frequenters. The back being entirely occupied with luggage, the two Germans, garbed with the dishevelled and semi-nude conventionality that characterizes modern sculptures of 'Youth in Industry', were obliged to coil themselves on pedestals of cabin-trunks and suitcases in those precarious poses exhibited by Michael Angelo's 'Dawn and Twilight', or the slithering torsos of Robinson and Cleaver's 'Linen Hall' in Regent Street. Gradually, as the carts grew more frequent and the volume of dust increased, they became but vague white forms, scarcely human beneath the livid coating of soft, choky powder. The effect of the municipal ornament was thus completed.

The level crossing at which they had mounted our hospitable step proved to be the first of a series of five in as many miles. The road and the railway seemed intertwined like the serpents round the wand of Hermes. In each case, we successfully arrived some twenty minutes before the train. And each time the gates were closed. When the train did come, the same fat man in a blue, striped shirt invariably leaned from the window next the engine, and guffawed at us.

Late in the afternoon, far away on the left, Vesuvius burst upon the view, surmounted by her little spike of smoke. No sooner had she taken flesh, than the correct umbrella-pine, leaning at exactly the angle most suited to this dearest of all the amateur photographer's compositions, appeared in the corner of the picture, and repeated itself with beautiful precision at every twist of the road, sometimes growing from a neighbouring crag, occasionally rising from a piece of marshy flat. Being a Sunday, the peasant women were out walking in great flapping starched caps of clean white linen, very bright, tightly-laced magenta bodices, and clogs. The sun began to set, its copper rays shooting fire over a flat mass of brilliant purple cloud. The mountain, the tree, the peasant woman and the glowing discord of the sunset, all combined to transport one into the stippled midst of a Victorian water-colour. One felt as if one was hanging on a wall, surrounded by a pattern of brown and pink chrysanthemums flecked with silver, and one wondered how the peasant woman had escaped from her glass dome.

At length, when nearly dark, we came to Caserta. The palace, as it was in the glory of the past, has lately lived again in the prose of Sacheverell Sitwell. Of its present he has spoken little. Built in 1752 by Vanvitelli, of a delicate brick, the colour of dying rose-petals, finished and coped with a dull white stone, this vast home of Charles III, king of Naples, stands a seventh-of-a-mile in length, 182 yards in breadth, and 125 feet in height. So perfectly proportioned is the whole, that at first sight it seems nothing out of the ordinary. Then, as the myriads of windows stretch away into a blur of dots, the immensity of the building strikes the eye with a jerk. Entirely detached from it are two curving wings that flank a wide, open space in front of it.

Far from apparent, as we drove past in the deepening shadow of the airless, August twilight, were the profusion and luxury of the tastes of kings and the vocabularies of authors. An atmosphere of decay, of desolation, a spirit of uselessness, of the body of a giant paralysed and unwanted, of the trunk of a fallen beech, pervaded the silent, uncurtained expanse of brick and window, the grand staircases to the main entrance on the first floor, and the peeling stucco of the empty wings. Situated in the centre of the town, the large open semi-circle in front of the palace was covered with matted, trodden yellow grass, From this there led for several miles a magnificent avenue broad as Whitehall, of dark-leaved planes, interrupted half-way down by a circular opening, whence radiated eight tributary roads. Directly across the spot where the trees began, the railway had

been laid, not five hundred yards from the central entrance of
the palace; and in addition, at this exact point, a large roofed
station had been constructed, with goods yards and sidings;
so that the vista chronicled by many former writers of travel
books, as the grandest approach to the grandest palace in
Europe, was now confined to shunting rolling stock, which is
perhaps less ornamental in Italy than in most countries. As a
final vindication of Italian nationalism the open space between
the wings had been renamed the 'Piazza Garibaldi'. It is said,
however, that there is still a Bourbon party in Naples.

We hurried past, the *Wandervögel* still clinging, and
circumventing the station, drove down the great avenue, despite
its holes. A few carts were crawling wearily along the edge.
Darkness fell. Our progress became slower and slower as the
dust from the harvesting wagons caught and deflected the light
of the lamps. Eventually we were brought to a standstill in a
small town, *en fête* for some religious ceremony. Squalid and
half ruined, it presented the appearance of a Luna Park, with
every building outlined in electric bulbs, and a series of tall
wooden frames that had been erected in the piazza, spluttering
with Catharine-wheels and sacred devices. Instead of the
rhythmic exhilaration of the merry-go-round organ, there
sounded the bored chanting of men and boys. Round a corner
came the procession, the priests marching past with supercilious
nonchalance as they swung their censors. Last of all was borne
aloft the image, that of a female saint, to the back of whose
head was attached a halo of small electric lights. The crowd
seemed mainly interested in us.

We had some difficulty in finding our way through Naples.
The view of the town from the hills above, a maze of dotted
lights stretching far out along the shores of the bay, soon gave
place to high houses and small streets, filled with a surging
crowd of chattering pedestrians and jangling cabs. David was
very tired and was thankful to pull up at the Santa Lucia Hotel
on the front, though aware that it was not the best. There was
no downstairs accommodation and the hall was filled with

the English professional classes. The *Wandervögel*, looking as though they had been dipped in flour, offered to wash the car out of gratitude for their ride. We suggested that they should go and wash themselves.

The next day we spent in a fever of agitation between Cook's and the garage. The garage refused to mend the punctures with the requisite despatch, and it was necessary to go once every hour to see that they were being done. Cook's had heard nothing from Brindisi and were prepared to make no effort for our convenience, until at last we sent for the manager, who proved more amenable than his assistants. We also paid a visit to the museum, but found it shutting as we arrived. I was not sorry. We lunched on the terrace of the Castel del Ova, that frowning pile of dark stone that rises from an island in the bay and dates from the Norman occupation of the twelfth century. It is joined to the mainland by a stone jetty and was not more than 300 yards from the door of our hotel. As we sat on the balcony of the restaurant, digging with delight at freshly caught languste, the view seemed to embody all the traditional features of the Neapolitan existence. Before us stretched the bay, blue and flat, with the huge town straggling away to a line of white houses on its furthest shore; and beyond, the lower slopes and furrowed summit of Vesuvius, rising to a little puff of soft silky smoke that dissolved into the sky like a bored summer cloud. From over the water, a fresh breeze flapped the white curtains above us, and the table cloth. The menu was expensive, the food good. Yet, immediately below us, the stone quays with their fleets of little boats, were proclaiming that fabulous poverty for which the town has always been renowned. The *lazzaroni*, whose lack of clothing was once a cause of '*une frayeur extrème*' to Madame de Genlis, are no longer. Their tradition has fallen on the fishermen and fisherboys, lying about in all directions and in all positions beneath the boiling rays of the midday sun. Old women, seated amongst baskets of marine edibles, piles of nets, coils of rope and rusting anchors, munched lethargically at their indescribable foods, in the intervals of begging from the passers-by. Groups of men were playing cards over bottles of red wine. Old sailors, their faces crinkled and deformed with disease, lay huddled in their rags upon the coping at the water's edge. The sound of a song floated up. On the left gleamed the long row of high modern hotels. Far out on the right the dim blue shape, as the ancients saw it, of a recumbent goat, hovered against the sky-line: the island of Capri.

There are few individual spots in the world that can have inspired such a multitude of writings and legends as this tantalizing rock with its inaccessible cliffs and its exquisite confusion of clustering gardens and forbidding mountain peaks. Who has not read of the golden broom, the roses and the wistaria, and the oranges dripping from their dark-leaved trees? Of the grassy vales and wind-blown uplands, the damp deep gorges, the weathered crags, and falling cliffs a thousand feet sheer to the peacock hues of the sea? Of the grottos, the villas and the miniature castles? History has left her touch: the bath of Tiberius, the castle of Barbarossa; the old red coats of the troops of Sir Hudson Lowe, the literary lustres of Compton Mackenzie; Marchesa Casati posed amid her bearskins; Gerard Lee Bevan disguised as Mr Smith; the Queen of Sweden in a green veil; each adds its breath to that siren charm, which so many outcasts, artists, and elderly women in search of adventure in small communities, find impossible to resist. Imagine it in the old days, when the Phoenician steps, cut in precipitous flights up nine hundred feet of cliff, were the only possible approach to Anacapri, when the tourist steamer was the exception rather than the daily rule. The siren of to-day, draped in a kind of aesthetic Union Jack, is the siren isle of yesterday, grown old with wooing.

In the afternoon I felt restless and plunged into the middle of the town. Naples is an alarming place. In the sunlight of the quays it may seem innocuous enough; but amid the dark shadows of the squalid tenement houses, the washing stretched bunting-like from attic window to attic window, the unkempt crowds jostling through the narrow streets and alleyways, some sinister current seems transmitted through the air. The poverty of the slums is no longer happy-go-lucky, basking in the sun. It is terrifying. The ordinary canons of decency are not observed. The day's toilet and the day's cooking are alike performed in the gutter. Many of the windows have no glass, some no frames. Children swarm. The whole population seems to suffer from perpetual sores and inflammations. The streets are paved with blocks of stone, fifteen inches square and six deep. Most are missing and the roads are consequently almost impassable, save when the tramlines serve as bridges.

I wandered on and on at a feverish pace, and at length, as it was growing late, boarded a tram, or rather clung to a handrail, in company with a struggling mass of itinerant humanity. The others thought I had been murdered. We dined at Bertolini's overlooking the town. During the meal an operatic tenor sang to the homely troughing sound of several families of Germans.

CHAPTER XV

THE DISTANCE FROM NAPLES to Brindisi is 270 miles. Beyond the environs of the bay, we were assured that roads did not exist. Conditions were bad; the road from Rome to Naples, though broad and imposing, had been insupportably bumpy, and we could only suppose that those further south would be worse. Moreover, the sun now began to set punctually at seven-thirty, and the darkness, when the dust obscured the lights of the car, made driving as slow as in a London fog. We were obliged to make the most of daylight, and were called at six, dressed at seven, and actually loaded up and ready to start by a quarter past eight. As Simon and I were waiting for David to bring round the motor, a youth passed selling English papers. We bought a *Times,* and in it found our account of the opera at Verona. This, and a packet of sandwiches thoughtfully provided by the hotel, buoyed our spirits.

Our way at first lay round the bay, past Pompeii to Salerno – thirty miles of practically continuous town, and if not town, cart-traffic and trams. The slums became revolting. Sunny as the morning was, wide as were many of the streets, the grey, fetid squalor of the houses, nothing but stone shells, the sight of breakfasts cooking in the runnel and the women emerging from the doorless doorways, hair loose and clothes in disarray, seemed to shut out the brilliance of the early morning, to create a sort of false half-light like the soulless glimmer that filters down a shaft with a bend in it. The traffic, streaming into the town as we were trying to go out, was directed neither by police nor by its drivers; carts, their owners either absent or asleep, dribbled in inextricable confusion over the whole breadth of the thoroughfare. Trams, filled to the roof with buzzing passengers, cursed impotently, unable to move backwards or forwards. To add to our difficulties, the surface of the road necessitated perpetual zig-zagging to avoid the incessant holes that threatened to imprison the wheels and smash the springs of the car. Even when the slums were passed it was no better, the roads growing narrower, the traffic thicker, and the holes, un-mended since the landing of Pyrrhus, being now concealed beneath three inches of thick white dust.

In the neighbourhood of Pompeii we passed rows of beautiful palaces in the restrained baroque manner of Spain – many set back among vineyards off the roads, with fantastic and elaborate entrance arches. Rapacious guides planted themselves across the road at the entrance to the excavated city. We passed on. Then the towns began again. Though to all intents and purposes continuous, each one impeded us with a separate *octroi* every eight hundred yards, which found it necessary to enquire of us whether we were importing or exporting long and unintelligible lists of provisions. One official at last had the effrontery to insist on searching the car and made an attempt to unload the topmost suitcases. Before he could lift them out, David whipped his foot off the clutch and the car shot forward with a bound that left the official half stunned in the middle of the roadway. Having experienced only too often the inefficiency of the Italian telephone, we decided to drive through the rest without stopping at all. This course, though alarming during a long wait in a traffic block, saved precious minutes.

By the time we reached Salerno, we had taken two hours to go thirty miles. But then, as we turned inland, the road became easier, narrowing as it ascended the mountains and developing at the same time a smoother surface, by reason of the simple fact that it had never experienced any traffic to disturb it. From now until Brindisi, 240 miles, we met one motor-drawn vehicle.

Rather than descend the most inoffensive slope direct, our course wound down the smallest gradient in a series of hysterical bends, so that even the carts found it quicker to go straight across country; and we followed suit, skidding gaily down the cultivated fields of dark red earth. When we were obliged to keep to the road, the bends were so sharp that David was unable to negotiate most of them without backing. The extent of our progress may be imagined. Nevertheless our average began to creep up from fifteen to twenty miles per hour.

About half-past one we reached Potenza – thirty miles short of half-way, a modern-looking town, filled with Fascisti on manoeuvres, and still decorated for a previous visit of the Crown Prince. We drove at a furious pace up the hill into the town, scattering the black-shirted youths; and were then told that our road lay below. The street was narrow, bounded by kerbstones nine inches high. Without hesitation, David backed on to the pavement, crunching the back light to atoms, to the pain of the surrounding crowd. We then descended and stopped at a garage on the hill for petrol. During the delay we opened a bottle of mineral water, hot and nasty from the heat of the sun, and made certain, as we had expected, that the sandwiches from the hotel were rancid and uneatable and also hot. We left them in the hedge.

That afternoon we drove through the most exquisitely beautiful landscape that it is possible to conceive. The country was not theatrical. There was none of the vulgarity of the sunset or the drama of storm and mountain peak. It was like a work of art, balanced and long premeditated in the soul of a celestial colourist. One felt, when it was past, that one had been vouchsafed an insight not accorded to other men – a vision of some pagan divinity, some all-pervasive spirit of harvest and maturity, of roseate golds and the red, brown, black riches of the earth of the south, the south of Hannibal and Magna Grecia, the cradle of European civilization. The countryside became entirely deserted. Long-drawn, sweeping contours of yellow and brown merging into the red gold of the August sun, that seemed to have communicated some of its own glow to this chosen land, rose and fell into the distance, disclosing here and there a range of glassy, purple, blue mountains on the horizon. There was nothing burnt; it was as though the colours

of fire were springing from the earth rather than descending
from the sky. The soil, where tilled, showed black and thick,
with burnt sienna lights. From time to time a flock of black and
brown goats would dot across the curving white road, herded
by a dog. An occasional peasant, seated sideways on a donkey,
would rein in to watch us pass. Above, the sky shone blue with
an unreasoning intensity. Few and far between, the towns,
usually on hills, glittered like clustering pyramids, unearthly
white and silver. And everywhere the yellows and browns and
the blushing golds: nowhere a trace of green.

We could drive very fast along the small white empty ribbon
stretching into the distance, and the faster we went the hotter
beat the wind and sun. Faces and hands grew a brownish
purple in the burning air. And over all clung the dust.

Toward evening we reached a flat and inhabited upland plain,
the now brilliant red earth of which was entirely ploughed. In
every direction stretched interminable groves of olive trees, not
the little immature bushes of the north, but trees, old, robust and
square, with twisted trunks and great spreading branches of grey
leaves. From among them, poking up everywhere in a most
unexpected manner, appeared sheaves of round conical roofs like
witches' hats, formed of grey stone tiles resting on the tops of
spotless whitewashed houses of one storey, with walls that sloped
outwards towards the foundations. As the roof was as high again
as the house, it could, if it was to retain the proportions of its
graceful cone, suffice only to cover the space of approximately
one room. Consequently a large and prosperous farmhouse
presented a whole crowd of these pointed extinguishers, all
varying slightly in height and shape, clumped irregularly together
among the olive trees, and each capped by a whitewashed stone
ball upon a stalk. The larger country houses were of ordinary
design, but invariably surrounded by stables and outhouses with
these roofs. One or two villas were adorned with modern Greek
vases and urns, displaying burnt yellow figures on a black ground.

At last we descended into the flat strip along the sea-shore
and found ourselves with twenty miles of straight Roman

road in front of us. This was fortunate, as we had hitherto experienced some difficulty in finding the way through towns, owing to the inhabitants' inability to read, and our being unable to pronounce the names of the towns as the natives were accustomed to hear them. The dust was now literally four inches deep upon the road. Men and women ran at the sight of the car and the choking blizzard behind it. Drivers of carts buried their heads in their hands with muffled curses. Even we were not spared. It came up in great clouds through the gear-holes, so that David was obliged to drive with a handkerchief around his nose and mouth.

As it grew dark we mistook some aeroplane hangars, apparently on fire, for Brindisi. Then we found ourselves the wrong side of the two inlets of the harbour. It was eight o'clock before we reached the town. A Cook's man, warned of our arrival, and a policeman, incensed at the absence of a back-light, leapt simultaneously on to either step as we passed down the main street. The fine was 25 lire. We had driven for 12 hours, with one stop for petrol, and the Cook's man was frankly astonished that we had arrived. After much-needed baths, we dined, and went to bed early.

Brindisi swarmed with mosquitoes, though they spared our faces. The windows of our bedrooms fronted directly on the quay, so that on retiring to sleep that evening, we found that the view had been transformed since dinner into an animate backcloth, punctured by the lighted portholes of a large Lloyd Trestino steamer in process of arrival. In the day seaplanes hovered gracefully above the harbour, noisy but decorative, with their white wings gleaming against the blue of the sea. It was too hot to go sight-seeing; the town seemed noticeable mainly for its smells. The Appian Way ends – or rather ended – here, in two columns, one of which stands intact beneath a luxuriant capital of sea-gods and acanthus leaves. The Greek influence is still predominant. To the left of the hotel ran 'Dionysus Road'. And the women still carry clay pots with long necks and double handles. As in Athens, reproductions of these in frosted electro-plate might be seen beckoning alluringly from the windows of the local jewellers.

We had intended to visit Lecce, the capital of Apulia. But it was too hot, and despite the praises of the town sung by our guide, who said that it was clean and that the inhabitants spoke Tuscan, we were so frightened lest some mishap should befall the car on the way and we should miss the boat, that we forbore. Lecce is the chief city of that baroque architecture rediscovered and given to the world by the Sitwells.

The frequent references to this family scattered through this book, find analogy perhaps in the homage paid by the past generation to Ruskin. But the Sitwell is concerned not merely to point the apostolic finger at Beauty in the abstract – which changes every twenty years with the mode in domestic decoration – but rather to leaven it with that lurking humour, which has always characterized the more exaggerated fashions in art, especially that of the baroque. The *serious* art-lover, the seeker after aesthetic *truths*, is blind to humour. And this fact, this unlikelihood of a wide popularity, will perhaps save the Sitwells from that tittering execration which is always accorded by the next generation to the favourite preachers of the last. For no humour can appeal as did the earnestness of Ruskin – can appeal at all – to an intellectual public that gollops greedily at the trowels of Bernard Shaw and Medici prints that are dispensed at moderate prices by the commercial disseminators of our national culture; that is content to hear its every problem, social, political, and religious, dissolve beneath the succulent paradoxes of the playwright; and that teaches its children 'art in the home' from tortuous representations of Peter de Hooch, just sufficiently expensive to add a substantial as well as an aesthetic value to the drawing-room walls. In the domiciles of the Brindisians, however, we were glad to note, each parlour has maintained its artistic traditions in the form of a tower of artificial vegetation under a glass shade not less than four feet high. We also enjoyed the vast plates of muscatel grapes with which the hotel provided us.

CHAPTER XVI

THE COUNTRY OF SOCRATES has no convention with the Royal Automobile Club. Under ordinary circumstances, therefore, it is impossible to land a car upon upon her shores without depositing a sum of money equivalent to·its full value. David, foreseeing this inconvenience, had, early in July, ventured into the presence of M. Caclamanos, the Minister in London, to ask his assistance in this matter. Did we, the Minister enquired, wish to disembark at Patras or Piraeus? David, thinking the former name less commonplace, replied Patras; to the customs officials of which port M. Caclamanos was kind enough to give him a letter. It then transpired that Patras was situated on the south-west corner of the Gulf of Corinth; and that only ships small enough to sail through the canal that severs the isthmus make it a port of call. On Thursday morning we awoke to find two steamers moored to the quay at Brindisi; one a large and inviting Lloyd Trestino, the other diminutive and dirty, with a repelling expression about it, like that of a small governess bent on a sartorial errand. This latter, the *Iperoke,* was to be our lot. While the Lloyd Trestino, with six hours' start, sailed sedately round the Peloponnese to Athens, leaving us to battle with three days' danger and privation on land and sea, in the effort to follow in her wake.

In the afternoon we paid a visit to the local Greek consul. To avoid repeated self-advertisement I may admit at the outset that all Greeks feel a personal pride in meeting a person bearing my name. David, who had gone originally by himself, was having difficulty over some minor point relating to the car.

He sent hurriedly for me. Rousing myself from an afternoon dose beneath the mosquito nets, I arrived in the consulate untidy and half-asleep.

'*Permettez-moi vous presenter M. Byron,*' said David.

The outburst of enthusiasm that ensued, the honour conferred on the consul, the blushes that sprang to cheeks as yet unhardened to such eulogies, are all too painful to recall. Every difficulty melted. Anecdotes of infinite length followed, relating to his adventures in a Ford car during a term of governorship in a northern province under Venizelos. Our parting was painful. Each step necessitated a lower bow and a wider smile, until at length the door was reached, and we stepped backwards out of his presence into the dazzling sunlight of the street.

It was now half-past three, at which hour Diana was timed to embark. With David at the wheel we drove sedately up to the side of the *Iperoke,* the deck of which was about eight feet above the level of the quay. The moments that followed were harassing beyond description. It was a holiday, and the whole of Brindisi was free to assist the operations. An hour's argument between us, the population, the Cook's man and the crew of the *Iperoke* inspired everyone with a thirst for activity. There was no wooden platform to which the ropes could be fastened, so that the Cook's man and the head stevedore insisted on tying them round the very delicate wire spokes of the wheels. No sooner had we by main force disentangled one knot, than another was being surreptitiously re-attached. Simon retired to the hotel embarrassed. David and I defended the wheels until a wooden platform was brought – or more accurately a rotting door.

This, however, the captain of the ship refused to take on board. The derrick, he gesticulated, would bear no more weight. Judging by the size of it, this statement was true. At length, roped round the body in a manner calculated to tear every vestige of paint from her chaste, grey torso, Diana creaked, heaved, and rose, one wheel at a time, into the air.

The whole ship seemed to list beneath the strain. Streams of agitated perspiration poured from the man in charge of the derrick, which was of that primitive type that can only be guided by hand. Even when raised to the requisite level, nothing could persuade the car on board, until the whole of Brindisi had clambered to the deck and flung its weight on the directing ropes.

Meanwhile, from the balcony of the hotel, the local notables looked on. In the centre of the town an agricultural exhibition was in progress, representative of Apulia. Along the circular kerbstones of the main piazza had been erected curving wooden booths, in the Taj Mahal style of decoration. These contained a succession of grapes and ploughs. A minister in a top hat was honouring the occasion, attended by a large concourse in morning coats and straw boaters. The navy was fully represented. And the Governor, a dignified bishop in slate grey robes, arrived in a motor attended by a tonsured monk with delicious pink feet. Three mounted carabinieri, plumed in red and blue for the occasion, sat like doubled bolsters on their horses at the entrance to the hotel. The lunch for forty, next door to the bathroom, smelt strongly of garlic.

At last Diana regained her feet, and half clothed in a tarpaulin, was used by the sailors as a table on which to cook and eat their meals. The garage had attempted to steal the spare tyres. The Cook's man went to fetch them, but returned with only one. At the last moment the other had to be retrieved in a cab, after having been extracted from the curtained recesses of the proprietor's bed-sittingroom. Eventually we left them on board at Patras.

Before finally leaving Brindisi, it may be mentioned that the proprietors of the Hotel International, where we stayed, were extremely dishonest in the matter of exchanging Italian for Greek money, robbing us of nearly six and eightpence in the pound. The American Express Company, in the role of whose agents they cashed our letters of credit, would be well advised to disown them.

We sailed, or rather chugged, out of the harbour as it grew dark, and sat down to dinner. The evening before we had taken a sailing boat and gone in the same direction to bathe. Simon, versed in sailing technicalities after his voyage across the Atlantic, had attempted to explain why sailing boats always travel faster when the wind is dead against them. The water was delicious, fresh and invigorating after the heat of the town. Unfortunately we had no towels, and were distressed when the sun sank with a jerk the moment we emerged in the hope that it would dry us. In compensation, however, the wind had changed, and as it was consequently blowing straight out to sea, we had come home like a bolt from an arrow. It was with regret that we now passed the scene of our frolic of twenty-four hours ago, imprisoned in the fetid little dining-room of the *Iperoke*. The food was good, and red and white wines were included in the fare, so that we ate and drank our money's worth. There was an American woman at the next table, anxiously making conversation to her neighbours, who could not understand her. She wore a dress of grey, imprinted with white rings.

Before starting we had purchased two deck-chairs; Simon invariably sits bolt upright. In these David and I sprawled on the top-deck for a while, gazing at the night and inwardly rather stirred at having actually attained the last stage of our journey, of being now certain, whatever might happen, of reaching Greece. About midnight we retired to our cabin-de-luxe, 'de-luxe' consisting of a basin and a tap, the only 'usual offices' on the ship. The heat and the sensation of claustrophobia were unbearable. Clad in pyjamas, I tiptoed on to the deck, and then into the dining-room, to the surprise and disapproval of a few fully-dressed men and tightly-corseted old ladies embroidered in jet, who were trying to go to sleep. I lay down and went to sleep.

Morning dawned to find the *Iperoke* at anchor in the harbour of Holy Forty (Santi Quaranta), a port of Albania. All around, large sweeping hills, more stone than scrub, loomed into the water. The sun shot a ray over one, then flooded the bay with light; the hills remained grey, misty and barren. The town consisted of a few big buildings, with stone cabins clambering up the hill behind. Eventually a lighter came off bearing a numerous herd of small, smooth cows. These were packed, like preserved prunes, on to the first-class deck, immediately above our cabin-de-luxe. Odd noises at intervals informed us of this. In addition to them, a number of live chickens and a family of cats with projecting shoulders combined to reproduce the more unpleasant characteristics of the Ark.

About lunch time we reached Corfu, and were obliged to take refuge in the dining-room from the swarm of itinerant boatmen and postcard sellers who infested the ship as soon as the yellow flag of quarantine was hauled down. As we purposely protracted our meal, the portholes became obscured by greedy heads, regarding us as their ultimate victims. Quite firmly we declined to visit the Kaiser's palace.

But peace there was none. The sultry calm of the afternoon, of the hazy blue water and the vague outline of the wooded island, was torn by the creakings of derricks loading conical baskets of fruit. A blind man and a *blasé* boy, each twanging a string instrument, came and treated us to the works of Verdi and Novello alternately. Behind sat the American woman in a basketwork hat. She had appropriated the chair of an elderly Greek of military appearance, who with his flowing white moustachios bristling against a skin the colour of smoked salmon, was not slow to turn her out of it. Then the vendors discovered her, and she soon presented the appearance of a stall at a charity bazaar, loaded with appetizing knick-knacks, native baskets, false amber necklets, poker-worked boxes of Corfiote olive-wood, and a positive confetti of postcards of the island from the south-west – and also from the north-east.

A German woman, too, gave us food for enjoyment. Very tan, and tautened in a backward curve rather than erect, her hair scraped back off an abnormally long forehead to show the ears, she trotted about the boat from man to man, stabbing each with a greedy pair of eyes and a succulent curl of the mouth that seemed to say, 'I'm a woman and I need chivalry. Give me some.' Her firm muscular form was originally swathed in transparent pink muslin, whence emerged a pair of shiny dark grey, silk calves, finished with dark grey suede shoes. For lunch she had changed into an olive stockinette tea-gown, with a sailor-collar and a slightly-soiled gardenia attached to it. Later in the afternoon she assumed a simple boating tam o'shanter of singularly hirsute yellow plush. Finally at dinner she appeared in a Napoleonic hat of black straw, sporting at one side a bunch of ospreys. The mole-coloured calves flashed their perfection of line throughout.

Eventually the loading was finished, and about six o'clock we began to steam along the coast of Greece. On the right lay Ithaca, overshadowed by two straining storm-clouds that seemed tethered to her like captive balloons. The mainland appeared entirely mountainous, meeting the sea with faces of rose-tinted cliff. Then it grew dark and we went to dinner. The American woman's conversation was still undaunted. Later we took the air, and were clambering about the rigging, when we found ourselves in conversation with two German *Wandervögel*, who were trying to beg a slice of watermelon from an Albanian shepherd. They had come on board at Holy Forty.

CHAPTER XVII

IT WAS SCHILLER, more than a hundred years ago, who first instilled into the younger generation of his countrymen that artificial restlessness which can only find expression in forsaking all and setting out upon a walking-tour. Under the disruptive influences of the immediate post-war years, with the fluctuations of the mark, the uncertainty of employment, the threat of starvation, and the consequent break-up of many homes, the vagrant impulse of every young German has been accentuated. Throughout the whole· of northern Europe, with the exception of France, in all the countries that once comprised the Austrian Empire, in Switzerland, and above all in Italy, these couples of bare-kneed, khaki-clad figures, dirty, smelly, golden-haired and, perhaps, but probably not, redeeming their sordid exterior by the joint possession of a guitar, are to be seen on all the large main roads, plodding through the dust of summer and the mud of winter. It is said to be a wonderful spirit that actuates them, the love of the earth, of nature, of mankind. In these days, the glorification of YOUTH in capital letters has displaced that universal admiration for MANHOOD which characterized our parents. And so these temporary negations of civilization are condoned, encouraged and admired. It is 'Wanderlust', say the young men; instead of becoming clerks, they set off into the unknown, chained to Freedom, carefully careless. With their spare money they purchase Baedekers and atlases.

A little time ago Cambridge scented a new era in this aged, but momentarily exaggerated, doctrine. A magazine bearing the word 'Youth' imprinted on a burnt orange cover, began a watery and vaguely improper existence. In the Youth movements of modern Germany, asserted this particular facet of Cambridge opinion, lay the only hope for modern Europe. To us, therefore, at a loss for occupation in the cat-, cow- and chicken-ridden interstices of the *Iperoke*, the two Messiahs out of Albania presented an opportunity to examine more closely this phenomenon that we had hitherto observed only at a distance or in print. We invited them to a bottle of red wine.

Their names were Herbert Fleischmann and Ludwig Schwert. Fleischmann was five feet eleven inches in height, with matted fair hair, a pleasant, broad, smiling mouth, and a long plebeian nose with a bulbous end. Schwert was short, but well proportioned, with dark hair and skin. His eyes twinkled and his mouth was elfin with a firm though protruding upper lip. He was Bavarian, Fleischmann Silesian. Both were clothed in a prevailing tone of khaki, varied with occasional knitted garments colourless with age and wear. Fleischmann sported a pair of laced field-boots. Schwert's legs were encased in Bavarian stockings cut short at the instep to display the tops of two brilliantly-patterned, knitted socks.

For four years they had been at the University of Heidelberg together. At a glance the age of each would have appeared to have been about twenty-two. Fleischmann, however, had served in the war for two years. Then at the end of his time as a student, he had spent eighty-four thousand marks on a woman in Breslau. 'Four thousand pounds,' translated David; while I computed it at four and six. In any case disaster had followed. On top of this extravagance the whole of Fleischmann's family, father, mother, and sister had followed one another to a succession of early graves. Schwert, the faithful Jonathan of old days, had come forward, and they had set off on their *Weltreise.* In England they would have gone out to the colonies. As Germans, the call to Perpetual Youth had transformed them into parasites.

Schwert provided the brains and resource of the party. This was evident from the overwhelming volume of Fleischmann's conversation. His sentences were pitched in a monotonous but authoritative key, like those of a guide to St Paul's. He was, in fact, a guide to his own achievements. His remarks were punctuated with metallic imperatives. '*Hören Sie!*' and '*Wissen Sie?*' and he had a habit of emphasizing his facts by wagging a forefinger in front of the bulb of his nose. Whenever he began to speak he gave a heave and threw back his shoulders.

They had already been away three years and they rattled off a sing-song account of their itinerary. First they had made their way to Odessa, and gone thence in a diagonal line across the Union of Soviet Socialist Republics to Helsingfors. Then, though ostensibly on their way round the world, they had come south. They were absolutely without funds. Schwert, in fact, had lately been obliged to have some gold stopping removed from his teeth, with which to raise money. David said that this was heroic. On the ship they had had nothing to eat all day, until the Albanian shepherd with pleasant smiles had given them some of his melon. Their plan, they said, was to land at Patras, and there find enough work to take them to Athens. David then offered to take them there instead.

This constituted a bond of gratitude. Like chorus girls on the ramp, they produced from their breast pockets photographs of themselves arrayed in their elaborately *Wandervögel* garb, and posed in manly attitudes before a studio backcloth of classical urns and foliage. These photographs form an important part of the equipment of every professional young German beggar. He can occasionally sell them, or accept charity under the pretence of doing so, thus avoiding obligation. Beneath the pictures in question was announced in almost all European languages the fact that they were going round the world. Fleischmann even boasted an armlet embroidered to the same effect.

It was indeed their real intention to beg, borrow or steal their way over all the five continents. They hoped to be home in 1936. Thus can Youth and Wanderlust convert into a haphazard walking tour the life of a boy and then a man up till the age of 35; and what then?

They drank about half a bottle of wine each, and this began to affect their demeanour. Fleischmann, with excusable pride, produced his stick, proportioned like an ogre's club. Beneath the knotted handle lay a silver shield embedded in a pointed wreath of bay leaves of the same metal, bearing an inscription of Gothic congratulation and good wishes for the round-the-world trip. The body of the stick was covered with deeply incised names, in all varieties of lettering and alignment. These appeared to be relics of the old Heidelberg days – the *Trinknamen* of the other members of the drinking-corps of which Fleischmann had been a member. Fleischmann's own had been '*Apollon*' he begged us to note.

On Schwert's stick, which was less like the bole of a giant oak, there were three names only. It was not difficult to visualize how popular Fleischmann had been, how mediocre the devoted Schwert. The couple reproduced many of the more commonplace aspects of the English public school.

They told us of their experiences in Albania. The Mpret or Governor of the country, a bishop, lately a waiter in New York, had at one period of his life had an injured arm cured in Vienna. The Germans had, therefore, pretended that they were Viennese; with the result that he had taken them under his wing and finally presented them with souvenir cigarette-holders, multi-coloured and square in shape, an inch broad, half-an-inch deep and four long. Of these they were forgiveably proud, smoking Simon's cigarettes with avidity. The Governor, they said, went about armed to the teeth.

Meanwhile more wine had disappeared. Though from all accounts a German university drinking-corps teaches its members to consume as much alcohol in an evening as a modern mother at a dinner table, the formality of our party began to dissolve. They started to play upon a mouth-organ and sing. Fleischman, infinitely the louder of the two, was neither in time nor tune. Schwert had a good voice and some technique. They sang mainly war songs: '*Der Wacht am Rhein*', and an anti-French ditty which delighted Simon, and made me angry. But the epic of the evening was a long-drawn ballad about a mother visiting her son in hospital and the son's eventual decease. This would have wrung tears from a stone in 1917. Even on the waters of Greece in 1925 we became thoughtful and serious; though the dramatic intensity with which it was rendered, would, in any case, have necessitated a demonstration of genuine and profound feeling. An elderly Greek asleep in a corner remained entirely unaffected, both by the sentiment and the noise.

The evening ended about one o'clock, after our having vindicated the Union Jack with 'Land of Hope and Glory' on the ship's tin piano. The Germans went out to curl up in our deck-chairs; we to our cabin-de-luxe, whence I retired to the dining-room. The cows were getting restless, and sleep did not come easily.

Such is the Youth movement in so far as it was brought to our notice. Both Schwert and Fleischmann became eventually very confidential, and the above facts are substantially true. Whether they are interesting I hesitate to say. Perhaps in days to come, the memory of this couple of young men, floating fortuitously over the surface of the earth, will serve to recall not only the miserable tragedy of a European war, but also the unsettled mentalities and bitter disappointments created by the Peace that followed.

PART TWO

CHAPTER I

AT FOUR O'CLOCK ON THE MORNING of Saturday, September 5th, the lights of Patras twinkled out of a rather muddy dawn, as the *Iperoki* glided into the mouth of the Gulf of Corinth. To our alarm, instead of mooring up alongside the quay, she dropped anchor 400 yards out to sea; and was immediately surrounded by a swarm of rowing boats anxious to disembark passengers. There followed one small lighter. What was to happen to Diana?

As the darkness disappeared and the mountain-tops began to take shape above the motionless surface of the water and the faintly distinguishable outline of the town, the black form of a larger lighter became apparent, moving silently towards us. This possessed a small deck at either end, perched above an uncovered hold in the middle. Gradually she drew up against the *Iperoki*. With the aid of the derricks the hold was first filled with barrels. Then the crew, joined by a host of swarthy stevedores, turned their attention to Diana. Fortunately the ropes by which she had been embarked had not been removed; and a second hour's argument was thereby saved. David and Simon were not present – or if they were, only in the manner of a harem, seeing but invisible. The Germans elbowed their way about, anxious to display their efficiency and make sure of their ride to Athens.

A fiery altercation ensued over the two pieces of wood that the Germans and I insisted should be inserted between each of the pairs of lifting ropes, in order to prevent their crushing the sides of the car. After an infinite variety of abuse and persuasion, two heavy beam-like boards were lifted from the roof of the *Iperoki*'s hold and appropriated to the purpose, leaving two yawning cavities in the main deck. The derricks creaked. Shivering all over, Diana, like an unwilling bull, was raised slowly by the nose, and continued thus until she was hanging at an angle of 60 degrees to the horizontal. With a heave, her hind wheels rose up on to the roof of the hold. There was a crash. One wheel had fallen into the slot left by the absent board, and the car came down heavily on the petrol tank, back light and luggage carrier. The Germans, assuming the postures of a platoon caught by a modern sculptor in its own barbed wire, flung themselves beneath Diana's body, straining every particle of their beings, muscles a-quiver, veins standing in relief. Sweat dripped from their foreheads. Paralysed by the horror of the moment, I was keeping aimless hold upon a rope attached to the luggage carrier, when, with a desperate spasm, the car rose again and threatened to swing right out over the sea. All that was to prevent it was the rope of which I was unwittingly letting go. The captain, choking like a master of foxhounds, seized my hands and transposed them after the fashion of a schoolmaster giving an inept youth his first taste of cricket. My feet he jammed against a beam. I was left like the little boy at the dyke, clinging like grim death to my rope, as the car swung helplessly in the air. Finally the off front mudguard crashed heavily into the bridge, despite the heroic efforts of Fleischmann to interpose his torso as a buffer.

At length, after minutes of suffocating suspense, Diana's hind wheels descended upon one of the lighter's decks. Then, very slowly, in the manner of a dog reluctantly ceasing to beg a lump of sugar from an obdurate mistress, the front wheels were lowered also. By some miraculous good fortune they, too, landed on the lighter. Faithful to the end, the Germans clambered down with them, while we went off with luggage and coats in a rowing boat, leaving the spare tyres on board.

Landing without having had our passports examined, we walked up to the customs house and presented the *douanier* with a letter from the Greek Minister in London. The effect was magical. Wreathed in smiles, the official waved our luggage past on the back of a remarkably active old woman, assuring us meanwhile that no difficulty would be made about the entry of the car into the country. There remained, however, to translate it to dry land. We marched in a procession down to the quay where the lighter was expected, the luggage on a hand-cart bringing up the rear.

No sooner had we reached the quay, than the luggage, which we had placed in charge of a small, peaky interpreter, vanished. Simon went in search of it in one direction, I in another. Then David disappeared as well. After a second exploration, I came back to find the interpreter resurrected, having deposited the trunks at his office. David and Simon were nowhere to be seen. Then the lighter arrived. Other schooners had to be moved. Eventually three rough-hewn boards, cracked with age and flaking with decay, were flung casually from the shore to the car. The Germans heaved, their countenances contorted with righteous exaltation. A crowd of loafers, half naked beneath a fog of rags, pushed with them. Up over the parapet of the lighter the tyres moved, then slowly down the creaking bridge and on to dry land once more. David returned; the engine started; with one triumphant bound Diana leapt like a gazelle up on to the promenade; then stopped with a grunt, from lack of petrol. A large crowd collected, from the depths of which the chief stevedore and the shipping company's agent clamoured for money. When petrol had been provided, we went off to the main hotel, which consisted superficially of no more than a door and a passage, and ordered breakfast in a café outside it.

Patras is a town sloping up a hill from the sea, at right angles to the quay-side. The streets cross and re-cross also at right angles. The buildings are all of that indefinable age and style that pervades the modern East – 'East' inasmuch as the Greeks invariably refer to their partners in western civilization as 'Europeans', using the word as a term of distinction. The main streets are arcaded. The stucco peels, without conveying an impression of antiquity. Most of the houses are characterless boxes.

As we waited for our breakfast, the sun gradually dispelled the early morning haze, and began to throw the shadows of the buildings upon the mud of the lately-watered roads. Looking down the main street to the harbour, the Gulf of Corinth was visible through a web of masts and rigging. The ships lay at anchor in hundreds, all brightly painted, in brilliant contrast to the piercing blue of the Grecian sea-blue into the depths, unlike the flat turquoise of the Italian waters. While beyond, rose the high range of mountains that embattle the further shore throughout the whole eighty miles of the Gulf, with wisps of misty cloud wreathing round their peaks like scattered thistledown.

Even at this early hour the streets were full of people, picking their way through the slush created by the water-cart. The modern Greek is of less than ordinary height, delicately made, and, at first sight, undistinguished. Both men and women, though seldom repulsive, appear mediocre and perhaps dirty. Then, on second view, the traditional type of the ancient Greek statue is often apparent, beneath a thickly-plaited straw hat and a small black subaltern moustache. The girls, though for the most part commonplace, are sometimes of great beauty, with nose and forehead forming an unbroken line, smooth brown skins, sensitive plum-coloured lips, and proud, rounded chins. The priests seem to tower above their fellows, upright commanding figures with long chiselled Byzantine noses and dark eyes flashing beneath their black cylindrical hats, rimmed at the top, their beards flowing down to their pectoral crosses, and their hair neatly screwed into grizzled buns behind.

The fustanella, despite its association with the Victorian geography book and the oft-told epics of pre-Victorian Liberty, is still commonly worn among the peasants. There is a certain unreality about any form of national dress, when seen for the first time in actual everyday wear One recalls the meticulous horrors of some Turkish massacre, purchased by one's great-great-aunt, from the Royal Academy of 1833. Or some faded photograph of a fancy dress ball in the seventies springs to the mind from out its gilt-bevelled cardboard archway. However, as we spread our tinned jam upon our rounds of dry bread, the dirt and squalor of the old men who passed by, their short tunic skirts either black or white, frilling out above their knees and their whole legs swathed in bulky white wrappings tied here and there like parcels of washing, belied any suggestion of self-conscious picturesqueness. There does exist, as a matter of fact a Society for the Preservation of National Costume. It has its representative in each town. But he struts about in full ceremonials, his white jacket elaborately embroidered in black, and a red fez seated on his head, from which depends a tassel that reaches to the small of the back. This has little connection with the ordinary utility dress. The shoes are large and flat, like barges, turning up at the toes, on which are perched immense black bobbles.

Thus we sat at small rickety iron tables upon the pavement in Patras, a prey to the fact that we were in Greece, when up walked two persons. The first was Mr Constantinopoulos, born at Salford, in Devonshire, the secretary of the local British consulate. He was dressed in white linen, and long flowing white moustaches projected on either side of his burned, haggard face. Simon, before discovering his name, informed us that his pronunciation was lowland Scottish. His English was colloquially Edwardian. He assured us that not only was there no road from Patras to Athens, but not even so much as a path.

The other newcomer was destined to play a larger part in our day. His name was Christian Teeling, and he had been born and educated at Dulwich. A small man, youngish and bald, with rimless pince-nez, he elbowed his way out of the crowd, and addressed himself to us in a voice of breeding and education.

'I see that you are countrymen of mine,' he said. 'Believe me, I shall be only too gratified to render you any small assistance that may lie within my power.'

He assured us that in these out-of-the-way parts a strange face, especially an English one, was always welcome. He was of the opinion that there might possibly be a road to Athens. He would fetch a naval survey of 1912, which would tell us for certain.

Meanwhile we drank our coffee. The Germans were ravenous and swallowed all the milk out of the jugs. Some distance away, at the top of the street, stood a castle on a high hill. Opposite, across the road, the shell of the old cinema, burnt down in the exuberance of the April carnival, remained. Posters of six months ago, advertising 'The Hunchback of Notre Dame', clung sadly to their boards. Mr Teeling soon returned. After consultation with everyone of his acquaintance, he was forced to confirm the forebodings of Mr Constantinopoulos. The survey of 1912, which he had very kindly fetched, supported him. There literally did not exist a road from Patras to Athens. The mountains shelved straight into the sea and the railway ran along a ledge cut from their face. Could we drive along the railway? Unfortunately the ravines were only crossed by trestle bridges. Besides, what course should we pursue in the eventuality of a train coming in the opposite direction? From Corinth to the capital the road was excellent.

Reluctantly, therefore, we decided to put the car on the train. The interpreter, in league with the hotel, discovered that we could not obtain a waggon that day. So we booked some bedrooms, brought out the Keatings, and with a 'so long' from Mr Teeling, who was a schoolmaster and had to be off to his class, set out to bathe.

The sun was now blazing at its height. With the Germans in the back, we drove some five miles along the road to the west. Then, since it turned off into the mountains, came back a little way. After some discussion we discovered a small strip of beach overspread with matted but sharp-leaved seaweed and screened from the drowsily-moving carts on the road by a row of maize. Why is it that maize is never grown in more than one row? The Germans produced red bathing dresses from their packs. Leaving our clothes in heaps upon the edge of the grass, we ran down into the water. After walking twenty yards over the tortuous weeds, the bottom suddenly went from under our feet, and we were swimming gaily about the spot where the battle of Lepanto was fought.

There is a unique rapture about a Greek bathe. The mystery of Ancient Greece unfolds itself. Those petty wars, those city states! Those burdens of the classroom! And now, lying back and blinking at the sky, defying the sun from the cool shadows beneath the surface, the endless succession of mountain tops, the foothills, half brown, and the scrubby olive trees, rocks and patches of cultivation, all combined to reveal the enigma of that legendary country, where Europeanism evolved in miniature and for whose sake men of all ages, ranks and riches, have sacrificed their lives in gratitude for their inheritance. The very air inspires a feeling of nobility.

We returned in time for lunch. I had trod on a sea urchin, and was obliged to assume a Byronic limp. Mr Teeling met us. The meal, which was served in a fly-blown restaurant with heavy, red plush curtains drooping round its windows, lasted from two to three hours. It was too hot to move. Mr Teeling informed us that, unfortunately, his wife was in the old country at the moment, else she could have entertained us. His quarters were limited owing to financial embarrassment resulting from his having started his career under the auspices of a Venizelist Government. Nevertheless could we bring ourselves to take tea with him? He had some roseleaf jam.

We said that we should be very pleased. At three o'clock David drove up to the station to put the car on a railway waggon ready for the morning. Simon and I sat in the street. We bought an illustrated paper, called the *Excelsior* – ΕΞΕΛΣΙΟΡ. Though published daily, its news photographs consisted entirely of portraits of international stage favourites and views of Japanese tea-gardens in spring. The letterpress we could not decipher. It is one of the fallacies most sedulously fostered by schoolmasters among their pupils, that modern Greek bears no relation to old. Both are precisely the same, though not unnaturally some of the more obscure grammatical forms have been dropped. I much regretted that owing to this deception, I had not attempted to preserve some remnant of a former culture.

Eventually we laid the paper upon our table, whereat the newspaper boys tried to snatch it away, in order to resell it. To Simon's annoyance, I tore it up, with cold-blooded deliberation, before their eyes. They then went away, but were replaced by a swarm of another genus armed with brushes and polish with which they were anxious to set about our feet. These in their turn, were followed by men carrying baskets of delicious-looking almonds, dispensed with the naked palm. At length, weary of the attentions of the populace, we went to tea.

The roseleaf jam burst on our palates like the Pacific on Bilbao's vision. Its taste was as rare as that of Tokay. David arrived before it was finished, hot, bruised and angry. The Germans and he had had to lift Diana bodily on to her truck, as the narrow gauge rolling-stock was only just long and broad enough to take the car at all; and the ends of the truck refused to let down. He finished the jam. Then we sat and talked. Mr Teeling said that his wife was enjoying her summer with the baby at Reigate. He offered us a bath, but as the water supply was limited, we declined to impose on his kindness too much.

He occupied the ground floor of one house. The rooms were small but lofty, and decorated with highly-finished modern Greek pottery and Japanese landscapes of Fuji Yama rising from between storks and irises, painted on rush matting. Strips of brilliant-coloured native cloth patterned in black, blue, red and white diamonds, and a Medici print here and there, completed the effect. On a table an expensively-illustrated edition of Shakespeare and a very beautifully-bound Dante in illuminated vellum proved our host to be a citizen of the Republic of Letters. After looking through some photograph albums, we walked out to see the castle.

The twilight was already deepening as we climbed the hill by a series of steps winding amidst a labyrinth of small houses, which gradually, as we rose higher, gave place to one-roomed mud boxes. Occasionally, as we picked our way, we would stumble over a strand of wire connecting two sticks, where someone had appropriated a piece of land – or more accurately a convenient shelf of hill – on which to build a home. Perhaps the materials were even in the making and the rectangular mud bricks lying out in rows to dry. It was at last possible to appreciate the embarrassment inflicted on the children of Israel by the absence of straw.

At length we reached the castle, David and Simon panting with indignation at being thus dragged to any object of interest, Mr Teeling the while maintaining a flow of interesting conversation. It was almost night. Across the gulf the mountains were just visible. Somewhere in their midst lay Missolonghi. Below, the myriad roofs of the town stretched down to the harbour, now a blaze of twinkling lights duplicated and triplicated in the ripples. A streak of smoky orange gradually faded in the sky. Suddenly a gunshot sounded, boomed and echoed from hill to hill. It was the salute of departure to the first boat of the currant fleet bound for America.

September is the busiest month of the year in Patras, when all the currants are brought down from the country and shipped to England and the United States so as to be in the shops by Christmas. When the first boat from each of the different fleets bound for the different countries sails, a gun celebrates the event. So rich is the land, that many of the currant exporters become drachma-millionaires simply by right of peasant proprietorship. Throughout Greece there is land awaiting ownership, though much has lately been alloted to refugees from Smyrna and Asia Minor. Still, If a man builds a house with a roof over it on unclaimed land, the land becomes his.

The castle of Patras is Roman, Byzantine, Frankish, Saracenic and Venetian, thus epitomising the whole history of Greek dependence. Groping our way in the blackness, we examined the Roman aqueduct, carried across what had formerly been a moat. In the walls the white marble of ancient Greek capitals glistened at random from among the blocks of stone. The lintel posts of one doorway were inscribed with Gothic lettering, and the cross-piece of another with Turkish. A Roman well-head stood in a courtyard, to which a carved Byzantine archway gave entrance. And the whole length of the rampart exhibited a typical pattern of Venetian fortifications, resembling the inverted pelmet of a cardinal's throne. The building is at present used as a convict prison;

and the forms of sentries motionless and silent, gave an air of
reality to the historic traditions. Mr Teeling dealt with them
in suave and fluent Greek.

We descended by the road. As there was a moon, the town
was not lighted. Gas is too precious to waste. Since, however,
the moon did not rise until after midnight, we were obliged to
feel our way as best we could over the irregular surface of the
road. We came eventually to an open square. On the opposite
side of it rose the face of a substantial oblong building,
punctuated by two tiers of barred and lighted windows,
behind which black figures were moving in spasmodic groups.
At a door in the centre, and at the lower windows, crowds of
women were swarming and talking in low, even voices. This
was the debtor's prison, a subject for a modern Hogarth. There
is no bankruptcy law for the poor in Greece.

Mr Teeling then honoured us with his company at dinner
– not upon the pavement but in the road. The Germans had
taken advantage of our absence to write some postcards home
– the first for months. We ordered a bottle of syrupy brown
wine, named Malvasia, first manufactured at Monemvasia in
Sparta. This wine, which we had also tasted at Ferrara, was the
original Malmsey, exported to our then notoriously drunken
island, in which the Duke of Clarence, whose bones now hang
in a glass case on the walls of the crypt of Tewkesbury Abbey,
met his unfortunate end. It is a strange coincidence that not
only did the wine of Malmsey have its birthplace in Greece,
but also the Dukedom of Clarence. One of the oldest titles of
the English monarchy takes its name from a small town on the
West coast of the Peloponnese.

Glarentza, as it is properly called, first assumed its position as
a ducal appendage, in the peerage of the principality of Achaia,
under the rule of Geoffrey de Villehardouin, the second of the
Frankish princes of that province. Later it became the chief
port of the Morea and the seat of the Achaian royal mint. By
the marriage of Count Florence of Hainault with Isabella de
Villehardouin, the title eventually descended to the counts of

Hainault; and was arbitrarily revived by Edward III and his queen, Philippa of that family, in favour of their second son, Lionel. The town itself was destroyed in 1430 by order of the then Exarch of Mistra, Constantine Dragases, future and last Emperor of the East.

As our dinner progressed, enough Malmsey to have drowned a hundred Dukes of Clarence seemed to disappear. Mr Teeling's complexion assumed the tints of a duck's egg, and he began to chortle out a series of naughty stories. I retired to bed early. The others sought adventure on the pier, where a jazz-band was playing, though no one would dance to it.

On our way to dinner, an English youth of about our own age had come running up to ask if we would play tennis tomorrow. He had heard of our arrival. His name was Sullivan, and his family had lived in Patras for over a hundred years. He himself had rowed for London University, and his elder brothers were also familiar with the Henley course. We replied that, unfortunately, our game was football.

CHAPTER II

THE NEXT DAY WAS SUNDAY. We had been careful to move the beds away from the walls of the single bedroom which we were all three obliged to share, and had also strewn little rings of Keating's powder round each of the castors of the bedsteads. We were therefore sleeping soundly when aroused by the porter holding a hand-candlestick, at half-past five. Dressing by the light of one gas mantle, set in the furthest corner of the room, we caught the seven o'clock express to Athens, the car, accompanied by the Germans, having preceded us two hours earlier. Mr Constantinopoulos came down to see us off, his gnarled brown hands twitching and washing in a manner that showed he had retained the English Saturday night tradition of his youth.

'Don't kiss too many pretty girls in Athens,' he croaked. 'Bye-bye – be good!'

The train moved off. We were ensconced in a first-class carriage, so small that it was unable to contain even our suitcases; a square box with one seat in each corner, upholstered in faded green casement cloth, upon which hung antimacassars browned with the contact of successive generations of heads. The ceiling was painted in a design of acanthus leaves radiating from the gas globe in brown and ochre relief. Above one seat was inlet a coloured photograph of Olympia. The old narrow gauge rails were no wider than tramlines. After every station or stray cottage at which the express thought fit to stop, a different ticket-collector, each more Anglo-Indian in appearance than the last, would insist upon examining our tickets. They came in couples; one down the central corridor, the other along the dashboard on the outside of the train. So that if one had wished to hurl oneself from them, opportunity would not have been forthcoming.

The railway crept along between the mountains and the sea, keeping the Gulf of Corinth in sight during the whole journey. We experienced at last the satisfaction of seeing for ourselves that the road would not only have been impassable, but was non-existent. It was not merely that the bridges were down. This would have been immaterial, with the rivers all dry. But in most places there was no more than a track three feet in width with a precipice up and down on either side. For all her agility Diana could never have negotiated ledges that were too narrow to support her wheels. However she would be waiting for us at Corinth...

Thus complacent we drew into a small station surrounded by fig-trees, under which stood one or two tin tables. There, in a siding, lay Diana, on her truck, motionless and forlorn. We waved at the Germans, who said that they had already been delayed an hour. Though she was timed to arrive at Corinth two hours before us, there was nothing to do but continue. We reached Corinth at midday, having averaged sixteen miles an hour. There we waited until six o'clock.

First we had lunch. This consisted of fish that tasted suspiciously unwholesome, followed by the proverbial mutton of the English public school, tough beyond belief, with globules of whitish fat crystallizing on its surface, and garnished with the inevitable and tasteless French beans. We held body to soul with a bottle of Mavrodaphne; though even this was hot. Mr Constantinopoulos and Mr Teeling had both concurred in telling us that outside Athens, this was one of the few good restaurants to be found in Greece.

After sitting erect on wooden-seated Windsor chairs for two hours, we decided that the longer we remained in anxious expectation, jumping to our feet at every whistle, the less likely was the car ever to arrive. We therefore marched out of the station along a siding and descended by a slag-heap to the beach, the condition of which spoke little for the sanitary arrangements of the neighbouring town. After setting the whole gulf awash with our ducks and drakes, we returned to the waiting-room. The atmosphere was insupportable. Each breath was like drinking from an empty glass. I gathered myself together and set off to ascend a hill above the town.

The Grecian landscape in August and September, but for the vines, currants, olives, and salad-green pine-bushes, consists either of bleached earth, merging into surface dust of as many shades as the egg-shell of the common fowl; or rock of the same hue; or expanses of matted brown scrub six inches deep, that was once vegetation. As I topped the hill, the view disclosed a brown plateau stretching away to a field of vines not more than two feet high. To one side rose the dark outlines of a cypress and a group of poplars. On the horizon the ever-present succession of mountain peaks stood out from the sky. Below the cliff, itself a dazzling puttied white, with a man seated sideways on a donkey riding up it in a cloud of dust, the mud-coloured houses of New Corinth fell away to the sea in rectangular blocks. And beyond them glittered the indescribable scarab-blue of the water, a blue that threw the remainder of the landscape into a sepia aquatint, and the sky into the pallor of a new sheet of foolscap. On the right the gulf ended in the Isthmus, slit somewhere by its canal. Old Corinth was not visible. Choking with dust, I descended into New. But that strange ill-defined smell that pertains to Greece was too overpowering – the hot dry smell of dust, combined with the more pungent, hotter odour of untended chickens. I betook myself once more to the waiting-room.

Another two hours we waited. Simon sat upright as ever on his hard chair, watching the lines. David and I slept full length on the sofas that flanked the doorway. Above us hung still lives in bloodless shiny oils, of the school of the master who decorated the dining-room of the Paddington Hotel. Casual men and women sauntering in for a drink, were surprised to find two Europeans fast asleep, and a third gazing with the fixity of despair at the burnished metals.

After six, I insisted that David should come and paddle. We had no sooner taken off our shoes and stockings and wetted our feet, when a cry of triumph from Simon, perched on the slag-heap, proclaimed the arrival of Diana. Her truck was, of course, placed carefully in the middle of the train which was going on to Athens. And it required half-an-hour's elaborate shunting in which to release it, each of the hinder trucks having to be moved by a separate engine and deposited elsewhere. Eventually, with the eye of the whole station fixed upon her, Diana was manoeuvred up to a small stone platform, covered with conical baskets of grapes. Then, by the use of every dram of our joint strength, assisted by the entire station staff and an iron bar, which the Germans had stolen from Patras for the purpose, we levered the car on to the platform. Fleischmann and Schwert by their efficiency delayed the proceedings as far as possible. Despite them, Diana eventually arrived at the cloakroom door, and once more was filled with our six pieces of luggage. The Germans, in order to make room for themselves, took half-an-hour affixing a trunk to the grid at the back. They had some thirty feet of rope with which to perform the operation, and were determined to make use of it all – until the box was invisible beneath a ruthless network of knots.

At last we started. We crossed the Corinth Canal, a narrow cut in the earth, with sharp smooth sides falling perpendicularly to the water beneath. The bridge seemed of no great size, and one might have mistaken the cutting for nothing more than an ordinary ravine, but for the extraordinary spectacle of a minute toy-boat steaming along beneath our wheels, which was in reality rather bigger than an ordinary cross-channel steamer. Immediately afterwards it began to grow dark.

For the first part of the journey the road, as is usual with all paths of communication in Greece, wound along the face of the mountains, the sea, now the Aegean, glittering sheer below. Greek officials in London had described it as a 'verry good road, but tveesty'. It was an *abominable* road. In one place we pulled up within three inches of a missing bridge. In another, a gulley some hundred feet deep, was crossed by a few boards flung casually from one side to the other, some of which were not in place. Diana, impulsive as ever, shot over on two wheels before any of her passengers had realised what was happening. The Germans were terrified and full of advice.

Our map marked the distance as thirty miles. When we had gone well over fifty, a glow in the sky warned us of our approach to the city, and we were overjoyed to catch our first glimpse of Athens a glitter of distant electricity radiating over a large acreage of sloping hill. With an intuition that had become a second nature, David, guided by the ever-recurrent tramlines, drove straight to the centre of the city and drew up outside the Hotel Grande Bretagne Lampsa, attended as usual by an angry policeman asking questions about the back light. Very tired, we hurriedly washed the dust of Corinth from our pores and walked up the street to the Petit Palais Hotel to dinner. The Petit Palais is in reality Prince Nicholas's town house and has the distinction of being nearly twice as expensive as the Ritz. To our delight and astonishment the first person to be seen was Michael, seated with a party of diplomats, and eating a plate of ham with an expression of sardonic dignity. We descended on him with effusion and bore him away, ham and all, to another table. He seemed slightly embarrassed. Simon's pearl pin, however, saved the situation to some extent. Michael said that he had been dreading this moment for six weeks, ever since David had written to say that we were on the point of starting. We replied that we had known that, and had been saving up for it. Michael, it was divulged later, had never really expected us to arrive, but had known that we had actually left England because he had seen in the *Times* that Mr David Henniker had failed to answer a summons for mutilating an ice-cream barrow in Ludgate Circus during a treasure-hunt. David explained that there was already a warrant out for his arrest when we left, as he had forgotten to pay a previous fine. He supposed they would not bother to extradite. In any case,

Michael with his influence, could smooth things over. Michael is in the diplomatic service. His surname is Trower.

The food was excellent, and we appreciated the forethought of the Greek royal family in having laid down the excellent hock that was obtainable. It transpired that Michael was also staying at the Grande Bretagne, as he had been obliged to give up his flat. The water supply had run out. And his servant had found means of terminating the lease by inviting, in Michael's absence, all the most disreputable women of the town to a gramophone party, which was so noisy and lasted so late, that the landlord, who lived next door, could bear with his tenant no longer.

In the middle of our conversation there appeared upon the scene a small man with finely-cut features and a neat, white, military moustache. His name was John Lennox Howe – a name celebrated throughout the Near East for its owner's business capability. He said that he had already been informed that Kyrios Troover (Mr Trower) was dining with Lordos Viron (Lord Byron) at the Petit Palais. David he knew, as David's family have interests in an obscure bank with various roots in the Balkans. One of these Howe was engaged in winding-up. He was concerned lest David should attempt to borrow money off him on the strength of it. He invited us all to go round to his flat, where we discovered that he was the author of the only existing book on Heliogabalus.

His apartment was on the ground floor, opening on to a walled garden shaded by a tree. He gave us Raki, a native absinthe, to drink, and also Cretan wine. David, who insisted on staying till three, paid for his energy next day with a fit of depression that almost drove him to take the first train home.

CHAPTER III

THE POPULAR CONCEPTION OF ATHENS is that of a high, flat rock, surmounted by an academic temple; beneath the shadow of which lies a town so nondescript in its modernity as to admit of no visualization whatever. Somewhere behind rears Hymettus, alive with the drip of honey and the buzz of bees. In front stretches the harbour of Piraeus, still connected with the main city by the ancient walls. And only last week Mr Gordon Selfridge spent three hours in the place on his way to Constantinople.

If all the private schoolmasters who deluge the budding intelligence of England with their snapshots, would in future expend five drachma (3¼ d.) on a bus or a tram to Phaleron, and then swim, camera in mouth, three hundred yards out to sea, they might succeed in correcting these prevalent opinions. From this vantage point it will be seen, in the intervals of avoiding the jellyfish, that the Acropolis does not dominate Athens. It lies in front of the city, rather to the left in the direction of Piraeus, where a group of tall factory chimneys are spurting a *panache* of black smoke across the other side of the bay. The temple stands upon its rock, very white and small against the dull, charred mauve of the hills behind reminiscent of those sugary marble models of it, that are frequently to be met with among what stationers are pleased to term their stocks of 'Fancy Goods'. But behind it and behind the town itself, a high conical hill, shaped like a mangled and elongated clown's hat, rises to twice or three times the height of the Acropolis. At the top glistens a tiny building, white against the heathery blue of the sky. It is Lykabettus, as this twisted eminence is named, that is the outstanding centre of the Athenian landscape; and it is during the climb to the monastery at the top, that the best view of the Acropolis is attained.

The ascent of Lykabettus is a physical feat to be essayed only in the evening, when the sun is beginning to set. Even then its accomplishment demands unusual stamina, as the Athenian twilight in August seems if anything more stifling than the blazing fire of the noonday sun. From all around the foot of the hill, now that the builders are encroaching over the plain towards Hymettus, diverge the long, straight streets of the town, dotted with slowly moving trams and buses. Above them, terraces, approached by steep flights of earthen steps, offer footholds to clumps of rectangular modern houses. From these a rocky path, the surface of which exhibits a jagged, vertical stratum calculated to tear the sole from the most hardwearing boot, winds upward amid a plantation of stunted yellowy green pine-bushes, edged with grey aloes, that are guarded by long untidy strands of barbed wire – their stiffened, pointed leaves reminiscent of the municipal gardens at Torquay. Within ten minutes every limb is aching with exhaustion; and it is impossible to resist the temptation to stop and rest beneath a red and white awning, erected half-way up in order to shade a few bottles of mineral water, that catch the hazy orange of the deepening sunset in·their pallid, green glass.

Although from this point the Acropolis is definitely below the line of vision, its pillars now appear in dark silhouette against the distant silver glitter of the sea and the dull flame-colour of the sky. Far out on the horizon, Salamis rises purple from the midst of the water. Over the city, laid out in square white blocks in the plain below, floats a vast pall of dust suspended between Heaven and Earth. The world seems to shimmer through a brown gauze. Between the town and the sea, three miles long, the great broad road to Phaleron Bay runs straight as an arrow from the two, gigantic pillars of the Roman temple of Zeus, that stand on the outskirts of the city. Along its edges are visible two rows of small green spheroid trees, broken by the sombre utilitarian block of the Phix (ΦIΧ) brewery. Meanwhile the lemonade is finished and the sun continues setting.

A party of unfortunate Greek mothers, dragged by the enthusiasm of their children, were slowly making their way up the side of the hill. Clustered above us on a promontory of rock, to which was affixed a wireless aerial, a group of soldiers cracked jokes at our expense. At length, in advance of the mothers, we attained the summit. From the curtained doorways of the little whitewashed church of St George that occupies three quarters of this geographical pinpoint, came the voice of chanting monks. In a converted side chapel was an old man selling beer. We gazed at the view until the light was failing; then returned to dinner. During the day the thermometer had registered 105° in the shade.

Having foregone even a glimpse of the dome of St Peter's, Simon, though reluctantly forced to admit that he had seen it, was determined to avoid the Parthenon at all costs. David, some two weeks after our arrival, was dragged thither much against his will one evening, lest he should offend the national susceptibilities of a Greek who had become a friend of ours. I, however, accompanied by Michael in a tight guards' blazer, beige flannel trousers and a check tie in the German national colours, devoted my second morning in Athens to visiting the most famous building in the world.

There have occurred, since the invention of photography, moments in the life of everyone, when the actual materialization of objects familiar in monochrome since the earliest days of the nursery, somehow produces a sensation of such unreality that the eyes of the beholder seem to play him false, as if imposed on by a mirage. Such a feeling, I must confess, obtruded itself upon my common sense, as our cab gradually approached the foot of the mountainous platform on which the Parthenon stands. I felt that I was the victim of a delusion.

Eventually the driver brought his horse to a standstill. We dismounted, paid our entrance and climbed the rough, marble steps to the Propylaea. Behind us and below stretched the

Areopagus, whence Paul preached, a long sloping hill of scrub and rock, culminating in a marble cenotaph. To the right of this and infinitely far below again, where the houses began and the people seemed to crawl along like atrophied house-flies, stood the temple of Theseus, to one side of a large, brown square – itself large and brown and square. Turning, there confronted us through the pillared archway of the Propylaea a broad upward slope of shining grey stone, from the crevices of which spurted little bushes and tufts of dead grass. Strewn in all directions lay blocks of white marble gleaming in the brilliant sunlight, their broken sides displaying the oldest, and at the same time the most modern, architectural conventions, varied with now and then a fragmentary bas-relief, the hindquarters of a horse, a human arm, or draped hip. And at the top, rising from its massive double base, there stood the Parthenon, the supreme challenge of man's hand to that of Time.

Looking into a shop window later in the day, I was unable to help noticing some typical water-colour sketches of the Russell Flint School, which depicted the Parthenon as a row of grooved cinnamon ninepins against a sky the colour of a faded butcher's apron. It is pictures such as these, reacting on minds already sickened by those yellowed photographs that invariably adorn the dining-rooms of British pedagogy – photographs enlarged to accentuate every scratch and chip into a deep and crumbling abrasion – it is these that are responsible for the loathing with which the artistically educated person of the twentieth century is growing to regard anything in the nature of a 'Greek Ruin'. Let me, for the benefit of posterity, pit my pen against the lens of the Victorian photographer.

The pillars of the Parthenon are Doric, plain, massive and fluted from top to bottom. They are composed of separate blocks of marble, three and a half feet deep and five in diameter, which, at the time of construction, were forcibly ground to fit one another, only the topmost having been previously fluted. Then, when the succession of blocks had become a pillar, the whole fluting was carried out by hand. The marble is still as smooth as vellum, its surface hard as basalt, its edges sharp as steel. And for all the chips and flakes and holes, there is that certain quality about this handwork, by which handwork can always be distinguished, be it on metal, wood or stone-a textural quality that renders every imperfection not only superfluous, but invisible. Picture these pillars then, with their surface of vellum and their colour of sun-kissed satin, rising massive and radiant from the marble plinth of the whole building, against the brazen turquoise of the sky behind. At their feet the grey slabs of rock and the wreck of the innumerable statues and monuments with which the whole Acropolis was once adorned; behind, the tall spike of Lykabettus rising from the white blocks of the town beneath its veil of dust; in front, the chimneys and promontory of Piraeus; finally the sea and the islands. Immediately below, the Roman amphitheatre, a trellis-work of heavy brown stone arches one upon another, calls to mind the efficient vulgarity of the civilization that displaced the Greek, a relic infinitely more incongruous than the tramlines and the factory chimneys. Even antique dealers in the Levant despise Roman remains.

Tucked away to one side and built below the general level of the ground, so that only the cornice is visible, is the Acropolis Museum. Eventually I visited the other museum that lies in the town below. Serried ranks of giraffe-necked vases of every height from six feet to three inches; interminable statues of Praxitelean youths eyeing their overfleshed shoulders; plump fragments of female busts beneath elaborately-ruched djibbahs; triumphant wreaths of beaten gold; breastplates, brooches and safety-pins; every detail of the art and craftsmanship of Ancient Greece is ranged against the curried red duresco of their walls. The contemplation of the whole is not inspiring. But in the museum beneath the Parthenon, with its small, uncrowded rooms and mural wash of bird's-egg blue, are to be seen the real masterpieces of Greek Art – those early three-quarter-length female portrait busts, popularly known as the 'Aunts', to which the paint with which they were once tinted, still adheres.

Though dimly familiar to the general public in the form of medieval English alabaster figures, the art of painting stone has proved, except heraldically, a rare and usually unsuccessful one. In the case of these Greek portraits, it is not easy to convey the delicate beauty of the flat, worn colour. There emanates from them none of that insupportable naturalism that characterized later Greek sculpture. They are simply formalized busts of aristocratic matrons, with delicately chiselled features, proud, pursed mouths, and their hair done in pig-tails that hang down over their breasts from either shoulder. The paint remains, faintly accentuating the features and adorning the slanting, upper borders of the dresses. One of them in particular has stayed in my memory as the possessor of a pair of faint, greyish red eyes, the colour of rain-sodden poppy petals, that appeared, for some reason, no more eccentric than those of anyone else. When next one encounters the misfortune, dragged by some self-informmg child, to pass between the doors of the British Museum, it will infuse new life into the dusty outlines of the Elgin Marbles, to remember that in their original state these smut-blown figures appeared in reality as though of parchment gilded by the sun, shaded with the weathered reds and blues of this same paint, faint and flat, yet alive with the marble beneath them, like the coloured illumination of an ancient manuscript; the whole supported by the huge golden pillars, with the blue, blue, blue of the sky poured over the top and down the sides and in between. Yet how lacking in taste does this appear to the refined modern critic. The mere idea of painted stone rasps on his cultured mental palate like the kiss of a middle-aged cat.

In one province of artistic expression however the Greeks have remained admittedly unchallenged. We have had our Michael Angelos and Donatellos. But there has not lived since the days before Christ a single sculptor who has ever attempted that masterly formalization of animals, which formed an integral part of so many of the ancient Greek groups and friezes. The English public is familiar with the crested horses of the Elgin Marbles; it may even recollect the illustrations of the

Minoan bull's head lately found in Crete. But with the one
exception of the single head of the horse of Selene in the British
Museum, there is nothing in this country that can give even
the faintest idea of the real genius that underlay the Greek
representations of domestic animals – domestic, because
whereas the ancient Greek lion is often little more than a
cylindrical poodle, it is usually the swine, oxen and horses that
seem to have responded most successfully to reproduction in
stone and bronze.

In opposite corners of a small, blue room in the Acropolis
Museum, are the heads, shoulders and forelegs of two horses.
Each has been caught by the sculptor at a trot, a delicately built
thoroughbred with a strain of Arab in his blood. Eyes sightless,
yet sensitive to every movement of the horizon, muscles
invisible, yet tightening and unloosing at each step, manes erect
and square, ears pricked forward, nostrils dilated to breathe the
fresh morning air – every particle of the stone lives. And yet,
they are wholly formalized; there is no 'naturalness' to detract
from their reality. It is to them and to the 'Aunts' that the mind
should turn at the mention of Ancient Greek sculpture – instead
of to fat Appollos and the Venus of Milo. This last is, indeed, as
the auctioneer remarked, 'one statue broken'.

As we descended to the inevitable mutton of the Grande
Bretagne, Michael pointed to a number of white slabs of stone
about thirty inches by sixteen, lying in confusion at the foot of
the Temple of Nike and covered with deeply-incised Turkish
inscriptions. At the top of each projected a kind of broken
excrescence on to which used to fit a carved, stone turban.
There were several of these lying about by the side of their
original supporters, shaped like confectioner's cream-puffs. In
the Middle Ages the Parthenon had become a Christian temple
to which all the greatest men and women of the Eastern Empire
had been wont to pilgrimage. There followed the four centuries
of Turkish domination, when the Byzantine church that once
stood within the pillars was transformed into a mosque. Then,
at the liberation, the Parthenon was cleared of its excrescences,

Christian or infidel. These tombstones are all that remain to tell of the religious usage to which it was once put.

During our descent into the city we passed the Forum of Hadrian, with its rows of thin, grey, broken pillars, as squalid and uninteresting as its namesake in Rome, where the cats congregate and play or sleep amid the refuse and oleander bushes. It is for the privilege of demolishing the houses in this part of Athens, that the American archaeologists are paying a million pounds to the Greek Government, in order to transform it into yet another wilderness of unintelligible foundations. The American methods of excavation are noted in archaeological circles. The Greek Government has driven a good bargain, as not only does it receive a large sum with which to build new houses, but also retains everything that is unearthed. Works of art are never allowed to leave the country.

While still touching on the subject of Greek sculpture, there is one bas-relief in the Athens Museum, which, having only been discovered in 1923, is yet awaiting universal recognition. It is carved on the side of a square plinth, on which originally rested a statue. Against a background of faint, dull red, stand four male figures, white and unclothed. Each is holding in his two hands a hockey-stick – not a travesty of modern perfection such as the old Victorian tennis-bat appears when unearthed from the upper attic – but an ordinary, slim, well-proportioned hockey-stick. On the ground lies a white ball. The two centre figures are represented in the self-conscious act of bullying, each about to give the second rap upon the earth. The others are poised anxiously on the lookout. Were it not for the absence of protective covering, the whole composition, with its attitudes of alert expectation, would present an exact picture of the modern game. If the Greek nation, with its dangerously ramified foreign policy, were only to advertise this work of art more widely – for instance, engrave it on their postage stamps – they could be assured of the support of the English-speaking peoples for all time. It might, of course, become known that 'soccer' has Constantinople and the Young Turk movement firmly in its grip; in which case future Labour governments could only be expected to put their money on Kemal and his proverbial wrong horse. Hockey has not the same hold as football on the acute political intelligence of the British franchise. Had the gods but played cricket…

That night we drove out miles along the seashore, winding our way amid hummocks and ditches of brown dust. On every side stood old twisted olive trees made weird in the mobile beams of the electric lamps. Eventually we left the car, and walking down to the beach, sat down in the darkness to undress. It seemed best, however, to wait until the moon had risen. Gradually its halo mounted above the black brow of the adjoining hill. Then, like some million-candle-power fire-balloon, the great plate of light came surging up the arc of Heaven. The water, hitherto black and sluggish, was transformed into a sea of opalescent silver, which clothed our bodies in a kind of phosphorescent accretion as they moved amid pools of light. Very slowly the sand sloped, and by the time we were swimming land was but a dark blur in the night.

Hypnotized by the languorous pulsing of the water, I lay full length on my back and gazed at the midnight moon now risen to its full height in the cloudless murk. In my ears the Aegean throbbed gently. The roots of my hair quivered in the keen, shivering water, black and soft and warm. England seemed very unreal and very far away. That morning a letter had arrived from home to say that cubbing had begun in the forest. And as the mesmerizing ripples rippled, the whole scene seemed to come to life. I could hear the sound of the·horn, the thud of hoofs on virgin turf, the voice of hounds in full cry. I could see the horses ploughing through bracken to their saddles beneath the dull, dark green, beginning to turn brown, of beeches at the end of summer. And here was I, floating about in the middle of the night on the further side of Greece. I turned over and shook myself; then swam to shore like a marine comet. David and Michael were already dressed. Next morning we all three awoke to a sensation of indigestion.

CHAPTER IV

THE ENGLISH TRADITION is more firmly rooted in Athens than in any other European capital. This perhaps is not surprising when it is remembered that Lord Elgin presented the municipality with an iron clock in lieu of the Parthenon Frieze. Unfortunately this incomparable object perished by fire on August 8th, 1884. One can picture the cuspidals and pinnacle of its airy Gothic fretwork, wrought by a hand inspired as Pheidias' own – more so, perhaps, since the latter was outside the Church of England – and one regrets the passing of the old English 'Milor' and all that he embodied in the eyes of an impoverished continent. There remains, however, righteously erect, the English church; and the Athenian can indeed count himself lucky in this Gothic masterpiece. It stands on a small railed mound on the further side of the tramlines from the Zappeion Gardens, and is built of granite, imported at immense expense into the finest marble country in the world. There is no salvation in marble.

One cannot help feeling that in aeons to come, when the civilization of Europe is as that of the Hittites and New York lies buried like a Babylon undug, the English churches throughout the world will have endured, lights in the darkness, symbols of the incontrovertible permanence of Henry VIII's second marriage. The austere Presbyterian at Venice, the 'tables' of chocolate and gold at Florence, the groined haven at Rome – of which city Metternich recorded in the twenties that it was one of the amusements of the natives to watch the English families, decked like Paschal lambs in Bibles and top-hats, filing every Sabbath morn through the Porto del Popolo to their church outside the walls of the Scarlet Woman – these will abide until the world's end. Even at Patras, the unmistakable cluster of Gothic stone crockets beamed suddenly upon us from the end of a narrow street. But our natural pleasure at this homely spectacle was marred by the effrontery of Mr Teeling, who informed us that his leanings to Rome had lately persuaded him to resign his position as lay-reader to a congregation that consisted, he said, of nothing better than a 'pack of bigots'.

But even more forcibly than the undying spirit of Protestantism, it is the Byron cult that keeps England perennially green in the eyes of the Greeks. The foundations of the national reverence for this most picturesque of nineteenth century liberators were firmly reinforced three years ago by the celebrations of the centenary of Byron's death at Missolonghi, in 1824. The party of English Philhellenes set sail in March for the Kingdom of Greece, to be greeted five days later by a frock-coated President, who had dispensed with the King by plebiscite the day before. The festivities were, nevertheless, strictly adhered to. A lady in Greek draperies recited 'Maid of Athens' between the pillars of the Propylaea, illuminated, owing to the inefficiency of the moon, by the light of two bicycle lamps, and supported by a massed choir. An eminent Greek professor, having missed the first instalment of the state luncheon, complained that Byron was not the only martyr. The representative of the British Government, poet and ambassador, fell into the sea on the way to Missolonghi and was obliged to retire to bed until his trousers were dry. Finally, a special issue of postage stamps depicted the Liberator, enveloped in a toga, exhorting the populace and priesthood of his adopted country to further deeds of valour against the Turk.

Statues and tablets are many. The most noteworthy is the group erected in the Zappeion Gardens, depicting Liberty propping up the dying Byron by the nape of the neck, and proffering it a bunch of asparagus. Another reminder of the warrior-bard is the recurrence of the inscription 'ΛΟΡΔΟΣ ΒΥΡΩΝ' on the rims of the sailor-hats worn by the little boys. I was jokingly informed, in fact, that if a member of the poet's family, or even merely a bearer of his name, were to cultivate a certain measure of self-advertisement, he might reasonably hope to aspire to high political office.

It was with this end in view that Howe led me one afternoon to the presence of M. Kokkinopoulos, the Director of Air Services. A young man of twenty-eight, he was, according to Howe, the eyes and ears of General Pangalos, the newly installed military dictator.

'The time may come when Pangalos will need a puppet king,' remarked Howe.

M. Kokkinopoulos was to be found during the day at his headquarters at Phaleron, near·our bathing-place, which was on the opposite side of the bay to Piraeus. Between the roadway and the water, adjacent to the row of cabins jutting out upon a series of quadrangular piers, was the aerodrome, and opposite it, the Zoological Gardens. As the animals were all starved to death during the Allied blockade of 1916, the gardens are now used as the official residence of the Director of Air Services.

Having argued our way past a sentry clad in a soiled white sweater and a pair of trousers, we arrived at a raised villarette, upon the steps of which were seated M. Kokkinopoulos and a colleague of benign countenance, with whom he was conversing. Howe was contracting to supply the Air Ministry with waders. Myself, rather dishevelled and bearing a vermilion bathing-dress, I was introduced as a candidate for the throne. I said that I had my living to earn. M. Kokkinopoulos, who was educated in Glasgow, and therefore spoke perfect English, replied that he would keep the matter before his mind's eye.

At this juncture a unit of the Air Force, uniformed in the same manner as the sentry, brought us some lime-juice, which we drank sitting upon a ring of unsafe chairs in the midst of an avenue of preposterous, barrel-trunked palm trees, which ended some hundred yards further in a circular iron cage like a bandstand, forlorn and rusting in the absence of its rightful denizens. When our drinks were finished we stepped across the road to inspect the aerodrome, which did not appear very extensive, though barracks, in addition to aeroplanes, were in process of construction. Adjoining the Botanical Gardens stood an imposing concrete factory with an outline like a row of·saw's teeth, which had been erected by the English firm of Whitehead's for the manufacture of aircraft, on the understanding that the Greek Government was prepared to order eighty machines a month. So far the Government had omitted to order any, and M. Kokkinopoulos playfully remarked to Howe that he had no intention of ever doing so; several, however, have since been built. After promising to lend us a pinnace from which we could bathe, we all returned to Athens by bus, arranging to meet later at the Zappeion.

It so happened that evening that David and I found ourselves in particularly high spirits. When we arrived in the dinner garden M. Kokkinopoulos had already finished his meal, but with exquisite courtesy he forsook his own party to join ours. David, embarrassed by an occasional silence, began to chatter like a watermill, employing those assertive extremes of intonation that have resulted from long practice in inflaming the local snobberies of Gloucestershire society. Every dish that we suggested was discovered by the waiter after ten minutes investigation in the *pavilion-de-cuisine*, to have been finished. Food did not arrive and wine did. The staff would pay us no attention. At length, taking the glasses from the table we hurled them to the ground in the hope of attracting the waiters' attention. Athens turned in its chairs. And M. Kokkinopoulos, who had been slowly enduring the tortures of a vanishing reputation, found this wanton destruction more than he could endure. He was obliged to recollect an engagement calculated to occupy the remainder of his evening. As we said goodnight, I felt discredited. Thus are thrones lost and won.

The nucleus of contemporary Anglicanism in Athens is the Legation, which is said to be the best building in the modern town. It was designed during the reign of King Otho by the architect Cleanthes, the foremost exponent of the Greek

Revival in the country of its origin. A plain, square house of coffee-coloured stone, it possesses an ornate cornice decorated with elaborate ante-fixal tiles. During our stay, the inside was undergoing repairs, so that the charm of the black and white marble hall, with its basin-fountain and double staircase, was somewhat obscured by scaffolding. On the wall of the waiting-room hung a German map of the Boer War campaign, embellished with a photograph of Paul Kruger. A Whitaker's Almanack for 1922 also occupied a permanent position, and eventually succeeded in imprinting on my memory for ever the incomes of the royal family, during successive waits for Michael.

It must not, however, be thought that these delays were due in any way to the pressing nature of Michael's diplomatic occupations. Only twice during our stay did a telegram arrive to be decoded. Michael's work consisted of informing the Chargé d'Affaires that he had found him a rug of the shade that he required, or that a rare bronze altar candlestick was being sent up to him on approval.

Yet occasionally some such missive as the following would require a moment's attention:–

> ESTIMABLE DEAR SIR,
> At first I beg pardon from that I have received courage and write to you.
> I am an unhappy 17 years of age and without work. I am alone in the world and now I live in my aunt.
> I know English and French and my desire was from Smyrna of going to the English Navy which I love. As it is difficult thing, I pray you make it easy and I will be kind to you. My address is: Alexandrias Street No. 32.
> With pleasure,
> A. COCARA.

Name and address duly noted by Michael.

At the back of the Legation, the door of which fronts on the

pavement, stands the English club and the offices of the various
English commercial companies, which are approached by a
pair of double gates and a gravelled courtyard. The former is a
many-windowed room, from the ceiling of which hang three
chandeliers and which has its chairs and sofas upholstered in
neat holland covers – like those who sit upon them. No meals,
but only drinks are served. In one corner is a piano. The walls
are adorned with portraits of King Edward, Queen Alexandra,
M. Poincare and two life-size representations in Indian red of
King George and Queen Mary. Sponsored by Howe, we
became temporary members. The outstanding figure of the
moment was Sir Frederick Inskip, chief of the British Police
Mission. The dangers of Athenian traffic had lately resulted in
such a quantity of casualties that even Fords were now fitted
with cow-catchers, fore and aft, and the government had been
obliged to send for a force of English police who might teach
the authorities how traffic should be regulated. By the time of
our arrival, 'Freddie's Police' had become a household word.
As there was not one of their regulations that David did not
infringe every hundred yards, our drives round the town were
not without incident.

Despite occasional differences of political opinion, Greece
still looks to England as her fairy godmother, and English people
are granted special privileges in the country. It was the English
colony in Athens, who, at the end of the last century, invented
bridge – a game that was played all over the Levant before it
spread simultaneously to England and India. But perhaps more
significant than anything of the estimation in which the British
are held is the current belief existent throughout the whole of
the Near East, that Queen Victoria left a million pounds in
her will to the first male human being who should successfully
accomplish the feat attributed by Herodotus to the mule of
Zopyrus during the siege of Babylon[1]. By such legends does
the lustre of the Union Jack maintain its radiance.

---

[1]Book III

CHAPTER V

OUR DAYS IN ATHENS passed with surprising regularity. The great moment of union was the midday meal at the Grand Bretagne, on which indeed the whole of business and political Athens was usually focussed. The Prime Minister and his wife might be lunching in a private room with its folding doors carefully thrown open. An Englishman in a white drill suit and butcher blue collar would rush in to say that the government had signed his contract; whereat a party of Americans at the next table would mutter darkly. Someone had seen the First Secretary at the — Legation the night before with Ida Kazanowska. Simon was still asleep. Howe was coming in afterwards to show us his new lamp. David was unable to eat the chicken.

'Michael, who is that woman?'

'Good morning, Robert.'

'No, a gin fizz for me, please.'

'Wasn't last night fun—'

'Waiter!'

'We must go there again.'

'Waiter, I never eat things with bones in them.'

'Hullo, Howe!'

and so on.

Owing to the tropical heat of the midday sun, these lunches were generally protracted from one hour to three. There was little inducement to go out, as all the shops were shut and the whole town deserted during the early afternoon. When at last the last grape was eaten, the last fizz drunk, our procedure was invariably the same. Filing out of the hotel bedecked with towels and bathing-dresses, we would plunge down the furnace of the street to the bus terminus by the University, squeeze our way into either a clattering Ford van or a long tubular French vehicle, the final word in omnibus comfort and beauty; drive past the old Royal Palace, the English Church, and the Arch of Hadrian proclaiming with offensive ostentation that this was not the city of Theseus but that of Hadrian; down the long road between the round, green trees, past the Phix brewery and the aerodrome, and eventually arrive at the wooden pier leading to our bathing-cabins, whence it was possible to descend by a ladder straight from the floor into the sea.

The water, without being stuffy, was so warm that it was possible to lie about for hours without feeling cold. Howe and I, detesting aquatic frolics in which we are always within an ace of drowning, and preferring the cool, clearer water of the main current of the bay, used to swim out some two or three hundred yards from the shore, then turn, and gently treading water, contemplate the view: the Acropolis and Lykabettus rising three or four miles inland out of the bronze haze; and in front, fringing the distant shores of the bay, the long, irregular line of factories and hotels, broken now and then by a team of tramcars of all different sizes tearing noisily along the water's edge, their white window-curtains flapping in the wind. Then an armada of jellyfish would come bearing down and terminate our reverie. Not far away a rocky islet, which had formerly been the swimmer's favourite objective, was now the haunt of savage octopi.

When at last it was finally decided to emerge, the recognized procedure, as in all continental bathing resorts, was to lie half drowsing in the sun and slowly absorb the heat of its supposedly invigorating rays. Personally I find no pleasure in having an adhesive saline film baked into the pores of my skin. The scientific bather, however, spends whole weeks face downwards on a splintery board in quest of sunburn. The human body being only occasionally beautiful, under such conditions it becomes, so it seems to me, literally repulsive.

Think, for example, what a parade of all that beauty, wealth and fashion can produce, the word·'Lido' inevitably conjures up in the imaginations of those whose holidays are spent at Sheringham or Bexhill. Yet it would be difficult, when viewed impartially, it would be, one might say, impossible, to discover the whole world over any single spot with the exception of a leper island, containing a segregation of humanity so revolting to behold as the bathers upon that overcrowded spit of sand during the last three months of the summer season. The beach of the El Dorado Hotel presents the appearance of a charnel-house: an infinity of bodies; men with stomachs to make Buddha blush, lie helpless as turned turtles in the effort to get brown. Women, rolling back their bathing-dresses, prostrate themselves to cook their vertebrae, already blotched with staring pink weals. Giant raw-beef Argentines, in doll's pants, play tennis upon courts the colour of their limbs. Ordinary English mothers loose their hair and lie doubled up upon the beach in mauve bath-towelling pyjamas.

But it is the sand that completes the picture. Wet and adherent, a dull, mustard gray in colour, soiled with the soil of a million cosmopolitan bodies, it clings in scabrous patches to every particle of the human form, befouls the hair, clots the toes, coats the limbs, lodges in the teeth, cracks the fingernails, and finally invests the body with an appearance of filth and squalor almost unmentionable. Such is the Lido, that mirror of beauty, that mattress of temptation. At Phaleron we were at least spared the sand.

David and Michael used to bask for hours among the strange crowd of emaciated youths and inflated tradesmen that lay about in front of the cabins. We eventually came to know all the regular frequenters of the place by sight. I can recall a German sculptor's model with a Greek body, Jewish nose and gold eye-teeth; a pendulous grey-beard in a straw boater; a youth named Toli who sported a monogram on his left shoulder; another in a black Phrygian cap of waterproof material, who always swam underwater; a crowd of insignificant men with Chaplin

moustaches and Greek profiles; and occasionally a family of
Levantine Americans, whose accents were excruciatingly nasal.
Apart from this miscellany, we made two friends who were,
even before we knew them more intimately, most courteous
and delightful. The first was named Constantin Komara, an
athletic swimmer and diver. He was a financier. The other was
named Sotiri Cartaliss. He was tall and upright, with soft eyes
and a soft voice, well-dressed, -read, and -travelled, and on the
International Finance Commission. One seldom meets anyone
abroad who is not either a financier or a soldier. Cartaliss,
however, had had a different history to most. He had been in
Smyrna in 1922.

To the man in the street in England, the name of Smyrna,
redolent of rugs and mosques and Lady Hester Stanhope,
denotes little more than a 'port in Asia Minor' – where a
slight fracas between the Greeks and the Turks took place
just after the War. Perhaps most illustrative of the contrasting
significance of the word throughout the Levant is the fact that
people in those parts do not bisect their lives, as with us, by
such phrases as 'after the War' or 'up to 1914' – but say instead
'After Smyrna', 'Before Smyrna'. Western Europe is unable
to realise that acid after-test of disgrace and disappointment
that the name arouses in the Greek. Nor is it easy to estimate
rejuvenescent symbolism, expressed in innumerable cheap
designs representing Kemal and the Crescent trampling on
the Greek Cross, that it conveys to the Turk, ever in need of
political restoratives. On the day of my return to England I
lunched with a judge, whose latter years as an advocate had
been largely employed in proving to an insurance company
that, as the damage occasioned by the Turkish entry into
Smyrna was entirely accidental, they were therefore liable to
pay full compensation.

'Yes,' he assured me between two mouthfuls of pheasant,
'the atrocities were entirely imaginary'.

I sat silent, astonished at what I afterwards discovered to be
a typical misrepresentation. Just as a murderer, called upon to

defend his life with the statement 'not guilty' presently arrives at as implicit a belief in that statement as in the colour of the sky or the king's face, so everyone will more or less place his belief in the alternative that suits him best. But it would be painful to hear anyone, whatever his views, attempt to defend the invaders of Smyrna to a Greek. Even a judge would be made to feel that his remarks were not only absurd, but in bad taste.

Cartaliss' parents had originally been wealthy: his father a banker, his mother a landowner in Epirus. We were discussing Smyrna one afternoon at Phaleron, and he stood looking out to sea. When we had finished he turned round, and with a metallic note in his soft voice, said:

'You talk of it calmly – can you think what it was like? We drove down the quay to the North. In the back was my mother, her face green, her eyes starting from her head; my father chattering, myself the same. We drove full speed, over bodies and through blood. We pretended we were French, otherwise we should have been murdered. You don't believe it. We got away in the end on a Japanese battleship.'

'You should have seen the refugees,' interpolated Howe, enveloped in a towel embroidered in pink crossstitch, 'when they came off the boats at Piraeus. I met them all. Some were literally naked. Most had not touched food since they left Smyrna and were picked out of the water – and some of the boats had been delayed six or seven days. I remember you, Cartaliss, you–'

'Well, I'm all right now,' interjected Cartaliss, cutting short the reminiscence.

Many people talked to us of their experiences; and though each had a different story to tell, all agreed that the horror of the massacre had lain in its terrifying unexpectedness. It was universally known that the Turks were coming; but no-one foresaw the barbarities of a seventeenth-century sack. It was said at the time that the Royalist Party were anxious to see the army defeated, owing to its Venizelist leanings. In any case their chosen commander-in-chief was mentally unsound, and instead of having been shot, ought later to have been exhibited in a cage by the Republicans. His favourite pastime was dressing up in female clothes. This example was emulated by the demoralised Greek Army, numbers of which, arriving in Smyrna in a state of panic, forcibly divested women of their garments, so that they might escape in them themselves from the fury of the pursuing army.

During the past months the Greeks had not behaved with outstanding tact to their newly-assigned subjects in Asia Minor; and the Turks had been promised liberty to sack, rob and murder, if and when they reached the town. Many English people refused to leave, expecting merely an innocuous two or three days' occupation. The Turks entered in the morning. Everyone went about their ordinary pursuits. Then the streets gradually became unsafe. Men were asked for money and if they did not give it, were butchered then and there. The ignorance of the Turkish soldier was the salvation of some. Jews who had lately been speculating in German marks handed over worthless millions to the illiterate plunderers and made their escape. The money-changers were able to purchase drachma notes worth ten and twenty pounds, for a few piastres. Buildings displaying the Union Jack were left unmolested. On the other hand, bodies of English officers were dug from their graves in the cemetery for the sake of the supposed gold stopping in their teeth. *This task was officially entrusted to special units.* Then the firing of the town started. Meanwhile the English battleships in the harbour watched. A dinner-party was in progress on the *Iron Duke* and the band was playing. Three times the sailors sent up deputations to ask if they might intervene; and three times they were refused permission. Representations were at length made, but the British representatives allowed the Turks to keep them waiting on shore two-and-a-half hours, and then met with no success.

As the flames spread, the crowds on the quays were joined by others fleeing in terror from the burning area. Like buffalo at a precipice, the foremost were pushed into the sea. A Greek described it to us. He had managed to send off his wife in a boat, while he was left. Unable to withstand the pressure from behind, he fell into the sea and swam on and on until he reached the side of an Italian warship. The crew of this pushed him back into the water. He became unconscious. The next thing that he remembered was awakening on a British ship. He found his wife again at Piraeus.

Thus it was with many. Some drowned, some reached boats. On shore the Turks were having the time of their lives. Sagacious politicians murmured that this was really a war between England and France and that France was winning. That night an Englishman told me how he had led his wife and child in from the country, stumbling over corpses as they groped their way. When it was all over, the British put their feet down and said that it must cease. The Greek quarter has since remained untouched – a charred and ruined wilderness.

It was the end of Constantine. They did not shoot him, because, as the English Legation pointed out at the time, he was already dying. His body is still waiting for permission to return.

But the most insoluble problem of the moment that faced the new government, was how and where to dispose of the million and a quarter refugees that had arrived in Greece, most of them in a condition of utter destitution. Proportionately speaking, it was as though ten million beggars had suddenly arrived in the United Kingdom: this, perhaps, gives some idea of the difficulties with which Balkan governments have to contend. The majority were spread over the country. The remainder, about a quarter of a million, were eventually established, with the aid of an international loan, in a large wooden town on the outskirts of Piraeus. Michael and I found time, one afternoon, to pay a visit to this settlement.

We went, of course, primarily to see Phyllis. Phyllis is one of those women, handsome rather than pretty, with a suspicion of a curl to the upper lip, who are always ready with some new story, that comes catapulted out upon the first breath of greeting; slightly improper, in the natural course of things, for English people abroad always lose their hold on lingual proprieties; and inevitably funny. Her surname is Forbes-Johnson; and, having no money, she makes a living by drilling unemployed refugee women into a shed and setting them down to weave and embroider at her looms. At the moment of our visit, she had just sold a loom and borrowed a hundred pounds.

The journey to Piraeus is most comfortably effected on the underground railway. The only means of obtaining a seat, and that wooden, is by travelling third-class, as first is invariably crowded almost beyond the possibility of standing. As the train comes into the station, the mob on the platform begins to crouch, like cross-country runners awaiting the starter's pistol. Before it has even come to a stop, the intending travellers have hurled themselves upon the doors like vultures on a carcass, kicking and cursing, now and then uttering shrill, bestial screams. When all is over, those who wish to emerge, do so.

The electric permanent way does not run very deep below the surface of the earth. It resembles the Metropolitan Railway out of London. After half-an-hour's ride, we forced our way out of the train on to the platform of Piraeus station. Piraeus itself is reminiscent of a second-rate manufacturing port in the north of England. Finding a Ford car for hire, Michael uttered Phyllis's address, and off we hurtled, bumping painfully from floor to hood through the length of the extraordinary mushroom town, in which the Smyrniot refugees eke out an existence on the pittance of a drachma a day that the Government allows them. Streets and streets of wooden bungalows stretched in every direction, though a few rows of two-storey houses were being erected. The inhabitants, of every imaginable age and aspect, many of them wearing circular Astrakhan caps and huge baggy trousers, seemed now, after three years' hardship, to be in a fair way towards attaining moderate comfort, if not prosperity.

Eventually we found Phyllis in her workshop. She showed us her stock of high-necked jumpers and modern native textiles, many of the latter being as beautiful as the old; then launched into a succession of stories about her expedition to the erupting volcano of Santorin, during which she had shared one of the few washing basins on the boat with four fat male Greeks, who considered her immodest. After locking up, she bade goodnight to her aged assistant, facially a reproduction of Lloyd George, and we returned by the way that we had come. The crowd in the train was even greater than before.

Previous to this digression on the subject of Smyrna, we had been bathing at Phaleron. By the time we were dried and dressed it was usually six o'clock, and the sun would be beginning to obtrude its blinding rays of coppered gold upon the level of our eyes. Leaving the pier, it was our habit to cross the road and seat ourselves beneath a shelter roofed with brown layers of exotic dried leaves, adjoining an ugly red brick house. Chickens in every condition of baldness and disarray would drag themselves among our feet through inches of hot dust, exuding a pungent odour which was intensified in the dry, thick heat. They were occasionally accompanied by a dribbling, snivelling infant, clad in filthy chequered rags. In this paradise we would each drink a mug or two of light beer and eat hard-boiled eggs and pears. Then suddenly a bus would come rattling round the corner. A hurricane of towels and uncombed hair would sweep across the road, obliging the wretched vehicle, which had just got under way, to come to a standstill amid paroxysms of coughing and vibration.

'Damn – only two seats!'

'No, there aren't – there are three.'

'Yes, but that's the ticket boy's. So many have been killed standing on the step that now they all have to sit inside – so like Freddie's police!'

'Well, you go.'

'I'm in no hurry – I want some more beer.'

'Well, you.'

'No, you!'

'I'm not going.'

'Nor am I.'

'Well, Michael, you and Robert go, if you want to go round the shops.'

'I must say I ought to tell the man about that triptych – and they shut at seven.'

'Yes, well you two go.'

'All right.'

'Goodbye.'

'Goodbye.'

And Michael and I set off in quest of 'antiques'.

CHAPTER VI

IT IS ONLY THOSE who have themselves faltered through life beneath its burden that can appreciate the misfortune of a mentality, which, at the merest suspicion of something secondhand for sale, is as absolutely unable to resist the temptation of examining it, as a cocaine-fiend of imbibing his favourite drug. It is not merely the pursuit of this or that particular *genre* of curio that urges the fly into the parlour; nor is it solely the mellowing hand of Time nor the romance of previous ownership with which the object in question may have been invested. There is more. The malady is another and a milder form of that splendid fever that lured Livingstone to Africa and gold-hunters to Klondyke – the fever that cries of hearts un-Christian and treasures lurking 'neath the snows – of the hand of a master mouldering below the gloss of last year's varnish, or the mark of a craftsman peeping from under some price-pencilled snippet of adhesive paper. To those who have acquired, perhaps been born, with this disastrous complaint, who fritter whole fortunes on unrelated bric-a-brac, and condemn their friends to champ the day in draught-blown attics and rheumatic cellars, each unexplored doorway offers the possibility of a hidden Luxor; each dust-grimed window-pane the glamour of a treasure-galleon. Michael and I have always been infected since our earliest days of boredom at a public school; he to some purpose, since he derives a small but regular income from his perseverance. There was a time when I attempted to do the same. But I soon discovered that monetary success must result from 'flair', rather than taste. My momentary effort was the result of a single piece of good fortune.

It happened one wet and windy March afternoon during my first term at Oxford, that a friend of mine and I, having forsaken the horrors of a river only too familiar in the bosom of a former Alma Mater, were wandering disconsolately along the golden privet alleys of the Abingdon Road, when a board, rising from amid the dead chrysanthemum stumps of number 184, informed our casual glance that Mrs Mary Cook being now also deceased, there would take place a sale of her effects on the following morning. In company with one or two prospective housewives, we wandered inside, curious to view the chattels of a house that was so ordinary as to be interesting; and were aimlessly engaged in fingering a set of engraved fish-knives cradled in cobalt satin, when the friend who was accompanying me suddenly fell through the floor. Though it was no fault of ours that Mrs Cook had permitted her detached and desirable maisonette to fall into this state of disrepair, a feeling of guilt led us hurriedly to seek the shelter of an upper bedroom. After listening to make sure that all was quiet below, we looked about us. In one corner stood an ancient, wooden washstand, the yellow graining of which had almost disappeared beneath the barrage of a century of soapsuds. And above it, protecting from the same menace the rows of formal tulips with which the wall was covered, hung a large panel of painted wood. Upon closer inspection this seemed, beneath its coating of dirt and soap, to represent an inferno, in the form of a cavernous fang-strewn mouth, round which were prancing a series of loathsome, human and beastish deformities. This was evidently Hell. Hence the picture's relegation to the back bedroom. Next morning, I successfully acquired it; and some days later sold it at a profit of 400 per cent as a genuine work of Pieter Breughel the younger. Such was my first and last venture as a commercial connoisseur. And having since become only too forcibly aware of my real inability to drive a bargain, it was with a pleasant feeling of security that I followed Michael round the labyrinthine antique-shops of Athens. Being personally known to all their proprietors, and having been responsible for a large portion of their summer's custom, he was offered anything he wanted at the actual minimum. Occasionally a dealer would have been saving some newly arrived treasure for his inspection. It was his custom, therefore, to 'go round the shops' every evening between six and seven o'clock. And it was for that reason that we had permitted ourselves to take the only two available seats in the first bus.

Not very far from the bottom of Hermes Street, the Regent Street of Athens, that slopes downhill from the foot of Constitution Square, lies the recognized 'antique quarter', popularly known as 'Shoe Lane'. This narrow, crowded thoroughfare resembles an Eastern bazaar, with its rows of awnings and dark, poky shops, on the thresholds of which sit either dealers and their assistants, or families at work upon some such domestic industry as cobbling. It has often been said that 'antiques' are the same all the world over. Those in Athens, however, provide the exception. They bear no resemblance whatever to the familiar harmonies of good taste and eccentricity with which travelled collectors become weary and disgusted in their search for new fields.

The classes of object for sale, though unique, seldom vary. Of Greek remains, which fetch high prices, there are vases, small and large, plain and painted; statuettes in bronze, stone and pot, representing both animals and human beings; and occasionally some work of art of exceptional beauty, that is unwrapped with trembling reverence from an old clothes heap in a darkened corner of the room. Such a treasure was the cup which Michael bought on that particular evening. It was of alabaster and in two pieces, having lain under the sea for two thousand years – of an exquisite proportion, with a colour of cream that has formed on milk and been left to stand and a surface pitted as a skin by smallpox, yet smooth to the touch as worn ivory. Then, more modern, there are the rectangular boxes of old chased silver which can be used for snuff and cigarettes. Many of these are fitted with under-lids, hinged at the end, covering plain sheets of looking-glass. Such a novelty would make a fortune if manufactured by a Parisian jeweller. Also to be found from time to time are sets of old gilded glass, relics of the Venetian occupation of the Islands – bottles, decanters, tumblers of all designs and sizes, and even hanging lamps made on the eastern model. Athens is the only place in Europe at the present time where such glass comes on the market.

One whole side of the shop will inevitably be occupied with shelves of stuffs and rugs. Most of the former have already been made up into native dresses. Silks, stiff and glittering with metal tissues, woven in patterns of foliage and stripes; velvets, hard and close-spun, of rich dark reds and blues with brilliant lights; embroideries of infinite detail and pains, often, like the ancient art of Rhodes, almost Persian in spirit; materials of every colour and elaboration; gold, silver, red on white, and black on white, old, modern, Victorian, eighteenth century; all are to be found heap upon heap, manufactured into every conceivable shape of coatee, stole and trouser.

But the great feature of the shops is the primitives. Though these are for the most part eighteenth century, the word 'primitive' best describes them. For a thousand years the Byzantine tradition throughout the Levant had never faltered. There was none of Guido Reni and Sassa Ferrato to influence the local iconostasis-painter. And until the machine-manufactured olegraph sprouted on the booth of the religious candle-seller, the primitive form of wooden body and dark polished face had remained, since the earliest days of the Eastern Empire, the stereotyped adjunct of religion. The enormous quantity of these paintings that exist is to be accounted for by the iconoclast rule of the Greek Church and the consequent need for an even greater number of representations of the celestial hierarchy in two dimensions, than in the Roman. There is small merit in most of them. Yet with the dull gold, sometimes lettered with Greek inscriptions, of their backgrounds, the red robes of their figures, and their stilted architectural settings, their decorative qualities are superb. And if purchased with a certain perspicacity, they can always be foisted upon the ignorant as 'the new primitive in the dining-room'.

Now and then, however, paintings of real spiritual beauty emerge from the dust and gloom. Such was that which we discovered in a newly-opened shop in Shoe Lane. The proprietor knew Michael by reputation, and, being anxious to obtain his custom, was obsequious to an embarrassing degree. His wife beseeched us to coffee; his son in knickerbockers heaped preserved oranges upon us; while his mother, bowed with age, tottered forward bearing glasses of that none too common luxury, drinking-water. Meanwhile the panel was brought out and wiped with a damp rag. There was revealed, fresh as it was painted two hundred years ago, though slightly chipped and cracked, the head and shoulders of a life-size Madonna. Down the midst of a polished oval of grey ebony, stretched her long straight-boned nose, like the visor of a Norman warrior. Beneath it, a tapering hand of the same shade and texture was supporting a Child against a draped robe of subdued scarlet. Behind glowed the thickest of gold backgrounds. Unfortunately the Child was missing; the painting had been discovered in use as the lid of a chest in the island of Chios. The proprietor was intending to return for the purpose of finding the remaining pieces. He thought that they were still there. He would know in a week's time. Then he and Kyrios Troover would undoubtedly be able to come to some agreement. As a matter of fact David was at that moment planning in his mind the construction of a green bedroom at Highworth, and rather fancied the idea of this Madonna hung against the curtains at the back of the bed – a gilded wooden pavilion of immense elaboration that he had seen in Rome. The idea seemed to me sacrilege.

In more important examples of Byzantine art, Athens is unhappily deficient. Those to whom this strange art appeals, the expression of first the conflict, and then eventually the fusion between East and West, between the geometric philosophy of the Syrian Monk and the naturalism of the Hellenistic humanist, must make the seven mile journey to Daphni in Attica. From the dome of the monastery church there gazes upon the beholder, with a kind of furrowed agony, the superb mosaic head of Christ Pantokrator, the eyes of which appear to possess a kind of uncanny film, due to their mutilation in the thirteenth century by the lances of the followers of Othon de la Roche, the Lord of Athens, who presented the monastery to the Cistercian Abbey of Bellevaux in Burgundy. But in Athens, when the modern town and its square blocks were planned, almost everything Byzantine was destroyed. There remains, however, the charming little church known as the Gorgoepekoos, that stands not far from the cathedral. This building, which is in the form of a Greek cross surmounted by a tiny, tiled dome, scarcely four yards in diameter, is ornamented with irregular panels in bas-relief, which are executed in the flat, delicate style of embroidery, and display as many pagan as Christian symbols. But of Byzantine architecture, despite the claims of Rome and Palermo, there is nothing of outstanding merit between Ravenna and Constantinople.

The opinion has frequently been expressed by writers and commentators of habitually restrained enthusiasms that the most beautiful Byzantine mosaic in existence must be the most beautiful object in the world. It is impossible, without having visited Ravenna, to conceive even a tithe of the feelings that can have inspired such a sentiment.

To a person susceptible to emotion, when merely a vision of the past is conjured up before his eyes, Ravenna, as a place, is perhaps more overwhelming than anywhere in Europe. To the artist it is equally supreme. Language has scarcely been evolved to portray the interior of such a building as the mausoleum of the Empress Galla Placidia. This small, cruciform building was built in the middle of the fifth century as a burial place for the empress who was the mother of Valentinian III, and had died at Ravenna in AD 450. On the floor stands her massive and typically Roman sarcophagus; flanking it, those of two

of her relatives. The narrow windows, one on each wall, are
paned with thin sheets of vivid, glowing alabaster. Through
this the sun, or simply the light of day, filtered into buttered
gold, strikes the million planes of the sapphire mosaic of the
dome and vaults, where flickers faintly an occasional figure
etched in deadened, lemon gilt. In the words of Mr Dalton, the
author of *East Christian Art*: 'the... interior, with its colouring
at once soft and splendid, and the mystical suggestion of its
decoration, ranks as one of the most impressive in the world'.

From the purely historical point of view, however, the
culminating marvel of Ravenna is the large basilica of S.
Apollinare Nuovo, built originally by Theodoric in the first
years of the sixth century, as the Arian Church of S. Martin,
and redecorated some fifty years later under Justinian, when
the building was converted to Catholicism. The present apse
dates from the late Renaissance. But on the upper walls,
supported by the two long rows of marble pillars, are three
tiers of pictorial mosaics that run the whole length of the
building. On the southern side there occurs at the western end
a fifteen hundred year old mosaic panorama of Ravenna and
her once famous fleet, in which is distinctly recognisable the
domed octagon of the fifth century baptistry of S. Giovanni
in Fonte, which to this day stands just outside the church,
not a stone or tile disturbed. From this, a long row of male
saints, with black monograms embroidered on their white
robes, leads to a portrait of Our Lord. On the opposite
side, starting from a picture of Theodoric's palace at Classis,
stretches a corresponding row of female saints, headed by the
Magi in ringed trousers and Phrygian caps, and culminating in
a Nativity. The whole is carried out in pale colouring against
the sour gold of the mosaic background. Over the door is
a contemporary portrait of Justinian; in other places faces
of Arian saints have been erased. Fifteen hundred years...
The organ was playing behind the altar. Suddenly by some
mechanical contrivance, it swelled out from the western end
of the building in addition. And then, as if by magic, the

far-off bells of the attendant campanile came chiming and pealing through the silver air, as though in harmony. The Magi pranced and proffered, as they had pranced and proffered since Theodoric the Goth had fashioned them to glorify the Indian summer of the disintegrating Empire; the male saints gazed across at the female saints; the female saints returned the stare of fifteen centuries. And up above in an unobtrusive corner of the green, squared ceiling, there appeared, in place of the expected boss, a date, in letters of gold: the twelfth of February, 1916; where an Austrian bomb, to the delectation of the saints, had continued history still. Ravenna, once the seaport capital of the Western world, now but a drowsy landlocked market-town among the flats, yesterday the haunt of Byron and the refuge of Garibaldi, today has not been forgotten.

CHAPTER VII

IT IS A CURIOUS THING that while the name of Athens, in her capacity as the custodian of the Parthenon, has spread to the farthest corners of the civilized world, in her position as a modern European capital she has seldom received even the most perfunctory tittle of recognition. The improving tourist, gaze riveted upon the Acropolis, averts his eyes from the body of the town beneath, as though confronted by an Aphrodite with a goitred neck. Yet panegyrics upon the physical beauties and atmospheric charms of the other lesser capitals of Europe have never been wanting. Who has not read of the glories of Vienna, that huge peeling Bloomsbury, or the splendours of Hungarian Budapest, a kind of Bradford-on-Danube overhung by a palace like the Piccadilly Hotel? From earliest childhood we have known of the *Times* correspondent in Sofia and the single hot-water tap in Belgrade. Madrid is full of pictures, Copenhagen of bicycles. Even Christiana has changed her name. Meanwhile the Athens of today remains as unfamiliar as Lhasa. Yet in respects other than her deficiency in Byzantine works of art, she does not lack distinctive features.

One cannot but suspect that the recent attempts of General Pangalos to emulate the petty puritanism of Fascismo by legally limiting the brevity of women's skirts, must have fallen on not altogether fruitful ground. Even during our short sojourn, a leading daily clamoured to be informed whether the Bank of Athens was a bank or an unmentionable resort. Similarly, the fashionable barber's of the town was not without its embarrassments. Fortunately the fattest of the female staff had fallen deeply in love with David only the day before I had found my way thither. Smothered beneath a striped towel, with the scissorman puffing cigarette smoke in my ears – preferable indeed to his breath – I must needs answer unending French questions concerning the health of my friend and the probability of his paying another visit to the establishment – a cosy little place, decorated like a maisonette lounge-hall in the modern French *intime* manner. Personally, when I have my hair cut, half the enjoyment consists in sinking into that delicious coma which the application of the scissors always induces. Here was no such peace. Fair succeeded dark in bewildering confusion, until I was thankful to escape unshampooed into the nearest café, demanding beer with such fluency as had survived from the ancient struggles of the School Certificate.

Cafés in Greece, as well as barber's shops, are unlike those of other countries. With each drink is brought a small meal of radishes, cheese on brown bread, slices of sausage, or bits of egg – each portion harpooned on a toothpick, ready to pop into the mouth. Disturbance is incessant. Innumerable vendors, usually children covered with sores, twist among the tables, dispensing prawns, almonds, evening papers, shoe polish, lives of saints and improper novels. The crowd wanders aimlessly along, as many as not dangling Kompoloios, tasselled strings of beads which are sometimes of old and valuable amber. These are Levantine rosaries, and have the same sedative effect upon the populace as chewing-gum in the United States. We tried hard to acquire the habit with a view to introducing it into England. Unfortunately our two-and-sixpenny strings of green beads were lost almost as soon as we had bought them.

The horses in Athens also wear beads – two or three circlets, of a coarse, light blue, strung upon the neck to ward off bad luck. And, as a result of the inexorable logic of superstition, the radiator-caps of most of the cars are adorned in a like manner, with tight little strings of the same charms fastened on the forefronts of their bonnets. During the last two years the cars in Athens have trebled their number, there being now as many as eleven thousand. For the moment, in fact, their import was forbidden, owing to the enormous sums of money that had been leaving the country in consequence of it. They are nearly all American. The population has increased in the same way. Including Piraeus and the refugee settlement, Athens now possesses nearly a million residents. At the close of the war, the number was only 300,000.

Athens calls herself the Paris of the Near East, and she seems in a fair way to fulfil such a destiny. Once the harbour of Piraeus is ridded of the anachronistic monopoly of lighterage, which, as we had been made so painfully aware at Patras, prevents ships disembarking cargo direct on to the quay, she may become, after Marseilles, the busiest port in the Mediterranean. Certain municipal disadvantages are being remedied. The electric lighting system has been placed under the control of an English firm; and the water supply, at present identically the same in quantity and method of transport as that originated by Hadrian, is undergoing adequate alterations. Yet Greek and foreigner alike cannot but regret the passing of the old order. It is said that in five years' time, with the introduction of modern comforts and good roads, tourists will have ravaged the place of much of its charm; and after the capital the country. Proposals had even been brought forward to erect a large, modern hotel on the top of Lykabettus, in place of the little monastery of St George; though the scheme was quashed by the government a few days after our arrival. It was the great advantage of our late summer visit, which made even 105° in the shade worthwhile, that we were free of tourists.

The most entertaining time of the day was usually after sunset, which took place about half-past six. We dined, as a rule, on the Zappeion. This is a large garden in the middle of the city, composed of groves of short, closely-planted trees converging on a hill, on which lies an extensive exhibition building, constructed in the modern Greek style. There are two restaurants – the 'Oasis' and the 'Aigli'. The food at each, if indeed there is any left, is equally nasty, cold and ill-served. One dines out of doors, either on the ground, deep in inches of dust, or upon the roof of a square white building, electrically blazoned with the letters ΟΑΣΙΣ.

One evening we collected a large party and motored to Castri, some fifteen miles outside the town. Here an enterprising proprietor had lately opened a building like a Swiss *châlet*. Dinner was served on the balcony, while inside the best jazz-band that we had heard since leaving England played invitingly to a floor of shiny, white tiles. 'We' consisted of David, Simon and myself, Fleischmann and Schwert, Michael, Howe and three Greeks named André, Angelos and Socrates, the last of whom was a native of Missolonghi. Several tables were joined together and we all seated ourselves with the determination to indulge proverbial English hospitality. As dinner progressed, the English colony and smart Athens, arriving by taxi-loads in mauve tulle, became conscious of an addition to the regular clientèle. The climax was reached when David rose with one foot on the table (and the remains of several wine glasses) to propose the health of King Constantine. Four cabinet ministers in a neighbouring corner asked hurriedly for the bill, scenting another revolution. Had not Michael promptly drowned the confusion by proposing the first toast that came into his mind, the government might have fallen. As it was, every lip was wetted in honour of the Irish Republic. Simon, to whom national rites are dear, crashed his glass to the ground behind him; and everyone followed suit; Michael blushed, and as soon as might be, hurried us off to a less-frequented spot on the coast.

At length, when it was past midnight, we decided to bathe – to the pained surprise of the Greeks and Germans. Had English lunacy no bounds? We rushed into the sea, waving greetings to the moon and pretending to be Rhine maidens. The Germans saw nothing funny in it. After drying on a single handkerchief, we all filed into the cars and motored back to Athens to spend an hour or two at the 'Griffon' before going to bed. This was one of many such evenings.

The 'Griffon' is the night club of Athens. It boasts a cabaret show, which contorts itself *aux Folies Bergères* from one till three. Thenceforth, and in between the items of the programme, the assembled company dances. It has frequently been suggested, owing to the halo of fictitious turpitude that surrounds the word, that a book dealing with the many hundred 'Night Clubs' that flourish in the capitals of Europe might afford amusement to the public. Yet abroad, with no licensing restrictions, with liberty to imbibe any quantity of the sweetest of bad champagnes the whole night long, any spice of excitement that is to be found in the expensive and respectable 'hells' with which London is infested, disappears. In any case the atmosphere of all of them is much the same.

One evening a Russian lady of figure came up to Michael and said:

'Have your parents gone yet?'

Michael's parents had visited him in the spring.

'Yes,' he answered, 'they have. How did you know that they were here ?'

'Aha!' she said, 'I remember your bringing them into the Petits Champs at Constantinople four years ago' – Michael having been in the Army of Occupation. 'Then I saw them in the street here. Your father is such a handsome man. I wish your mother had not been here. I would have made love to him.'

The 'Griffon' was the ideal night club. Entrance was free; champagne was not compulsory. We passed many evenings there.

Down at Phaleron was a restaurant kept by a gigantic Cretan, and known as 'Cretikos', which was situated on an earthen promontory lapped by the waves. It was lit by one gas-flare. Each table stood in a cubicle formed by banks of earth. Fish in Athens is so scarce that restaurants are only allowed to serve it every other day, in order that the private consumer may occasionally have a chance of obtaining some. At 'Cretikos' it was always available. We ordered dish after dish and helped cook it ourselves over a grid.

Seated in the weird half-light of the gas, with the white edges of the waves lapping the sun-baked, earthen platform at our feet and the lights of Piraeus twinkling from beyond the blackness of the bay, we talked of Almae Matres, as we picked the spines of the last remaining red mullets. Michael told how a house-master named Parratt was once sitting quietly with his pupils, when it was suddenly announced that the kitchen-maid had been found murdered. Commotion ensued, until Parratt, who had momentarily left the room in order to view the body, closed the incident with the following words: 'After this somewhat vulgar interruption, we will now resume the ordinary course of our studies.'

A story supremely illustrative of mentality of the militant pedagogue, was that of Simon, whose tutor was named. Macveagh. A certain distinguished member of the school staff who had climbed to success on a mixture of bad aesthetics and Christianity – 'Faith is such a jolly thing,' he once told a batch of confirmation candidates – found reason, on one occasion, to complain of the unorthodox in Simon's scriptural studies. That evening Macveagh stalked into the room, gave a sniff like a witch-doctor scenting a heresy, and with an air of enraged triumph, solemnly confiscated the large collection of the works of Shaw and Wells, which Simon, even at the age of seventeen, was already beginning to find sadly conventional. It is thus that Youth must contend with Age, and is driven to exaggerate its follies in revenge.

CHAPTER VIII

THERE IS AN ANCIENT JOKE, originally evolved by du Maurier out of 'Drawing-room Theatricals', which consists of the following dialogue:

'May I enquire, madam, whether you believe that the rights of men and women should be equal?'

'Certainly, sir, I do.'

'In that case, I do not feel called upon to relinquish my seat.' Nor does he do so.

Though there is still something rather shocking in such an attitude, it must be admitted that the twentieth century has witnessed a certain tendency towards the decline of chivalric relationships. And in the case of the hardened traveller, this is largely due to the manner in which young American girls, with an independence of manner that is the reverse of appealing, make a habit of ordering casual males to attend their needs on boats and trains without even vouchsafing them either a 'please' or a 'thank you'. Unless, of course, the time is propitious to further the acquaintanceship. Then we begin to relent towards what appears to be on the surface merely a weaker sex trading on its weakness.

The reports that arrive from the United States themselves are so conflicting that one is sometimes left in doubt as to how far the accepted doctrines of modern civilization with regard to female emancipation have taken root in that country. And it came as a pleasant surprise to us during our tour, to view from personal observation the progress that at any rate a section of American womanhood has made toward moral equality with man.

The reader may have noticed that it was one of our amusements to make a comparative study of 'nightlife' – if an expression so distorted can convey the pallor of the usual continental, after-dinner entertainments. In Berlin, Salzburg, Rome and Athens, in connection with Panama, Calcutta and Atlantic liners, and finally *á propos even of Paris,* came always the same response to our ever-repeated enquiry for the local cabaret or dance-hall.

'No need to bother about that sort of thing here; the place is full of American girls. I can easily fix you up...' Or, if the speaker were indulging in a reminiscence, his reply was in the past tense. And thus: with characteristic efficiency, does our American cousin compensate the Universe for her lack of manners.

But the anecdote of du Maurier's old gentleman was intended originally to introduce the particular satisfaction of David, Michael and myself at learning of the successful assassination of one of the more mature transatlantic feminists – a Mrs Cook. We had planned one Friday to visit Sunium; and while waiting amid a crowd of iced lemon squashes for the motor to arrive, we chanced on this item of news in the pages of the *Christian Science Monitor* – the only journal which the management of the hotel appeared to consider suitable for the perusal of its English-speaking visitors. Mrs Cook, it appeared, had been the leader of her local prohibition movement; and was sitting one day at her window, when a party of bootleggers, with whose living she had been interfering, walked round the corner and shot her dead. We remember, at the moment of Nurse Cavell's demise, being deeply stirred; as indeed have been the most confirmed misogynists since her reincarnation from the hand of Sir George Frampton. On the other hand, we were and still are in the seventh heaven of felicity at the fate of Mrs Cook. The reason perhaps is that whereas the action of the Germans was no doubt technically correct, that of the bootleggers had no justification of any kind. Undaunted by legal forms they unostentatiously effected the removal of a busybody, trading, like her globe-trotting sisters, on the alleged weakness of her sex.

It must not, however, be lost sight of that Athens also offers possibilities in this direction. A certain Dutch resident had only a few months before our arrival purchased an expensive Greek head that proved to be a forgery. His servant, an intimate of the underworld of Constantinople, immediately placed at his disposal a number of hired assassins. And the dealer who had sold the head was very soon blackmailed by violence into returning practically the whole sum that he had originally been paid for it. To put it in commercial terms, a cleanly executed murder, involving no risk of detection to the instigator, costs in the neighbourhood of £25. Shall American bootleggers put us Britishers to shame? When, therefore, the newspapers announce that Viscountess Astor for example, has mysteriously disappeared, after being last seen on the Acropolis in a smart, navy blue costume, the restricted public that has read this book will feel no surprise. Precautions have been taken to prevent the above paragraph's reaching the eyes of our intended victim.

The drive to Sunium, some thirty miles in length, presented, for Greece, a utilitarian appearance. I was suffering from a cold at the time, which, in the intense heat, made me feel as though my head were a live bomb, about to explode. After driving twenty miles we reached a manufacturing town named Lavrion. It seemed odd to see the chimneys and mining paraphernalia of a Yorkshire slagheap, standing out of the seared brown hills against the unmistakeably Greek blue of the Aegean. In the central square of the place, which was no larger than a small English county town, the mines being for the most part disused, we lunched. At least we entered a small room on the pavement, already tenanted by three other groups of men and women. After half-an-hour's patience, we were favoured with a few small wedges of toughened flesh, together with a bottle of Mavrodaphne and three soup-plates of pink grapes. A dog – the only sociable dog in Europe of uncertain genus – enlivened the meal by his friendliness. On the wall hung some oil-paintings of oranges. The cutlery was coated with that sinister slime that results from too little washing-up water. We sat on drinking, loath to face the heat, and watching a group of local notables, who, in the company of their priest, were doing the same.

At length, about three o'clock, we re-entered the motor. The road skirted along the coast. Every now and then a small stucco villa would appear, usually of one storey, probably pink in colour. These were varied with mere sheds, and sometimes only shelters of boughs, in which families might be seen enjoying their summer holiday in the traditional manner. Outside some stood cars, momentarily providing additional accommodation.

Eventually we turned off to the left up a track which led us out upon a headland of rock and heather and little, scrubby ground-bushes. At the top of a long slope, on a levelled platform of rock, stood the temple that we had come to see. Unlike the Acropolis, the marble was gleaming pure liquid white with such intensity that its background of sky seemed to lose all colour, and function simply as a tone. The ruin is old, even for Greece, and very worn. The position is magnificent: sheer below on the further side is the sea, two hundred feet down. Unfortunately the surrounding country is being spoilt – at least the coast. It is the favourite resort of Athenians; and visible from the temple was a hotel already in the building. I concealed the fact from Michael, who loves the place, but I felt not altogether happy. Perhaps it was my cold.

At close quarters the most noticeable feature of the noble skeleton is the profusion of carved names with which it is adorned. At some obscure date a party of English blue-jackets had even borne hither a pot of tar whereby to convey themselves to posterity; in which object they have succeeded, as it is impossible to rid the marble of the stain. It is pleasant, too, to think how Mr Wilson, of Hull, must have enjoyed his visit here in 1875; and how Mr Schofield, of Burton-on- Trent,

followed in his footsteps fourteen years later. One may laugh
– one may deplore them. Yet in reality, despite the vandalism
and irreverence of which they seem symbolic, there is often
something strangely touching about the names that are to be
found on ancient monuments. It is a primitive rather than a
vulgar instinct that impels the cutting of them. They imply
not self-advertisement but a deep-felt appreciation of the spot
itself and an honest pride in having visited it. Untrained to
such rare emotions, the mind of the Hull shipping magnate
bursts to express them; spontaneously he writes:

F.A. WILSON, HULL '75

Excitement, too, is always especially visible in the pencil
scrawls that invariably decorate the masonry towards the
tops of towers. How vividly can one picture the spectacle of
Florence and Sydney Pike on their honeymoon in 1908, giggling
and screeching to one another in the pitchy darkness of the
winding stairs; bumping from wall to wall; squealing, panting,
sobbing; Florence treading on Sydney's fingers, Sydney
pinching Florence's calves; then suddenly both confronted by
the view – eighty miles to a mountainous horizon.
   'Ah, you should see Dartmoor, where Auntie went last year–'
   'Give us your pencil, Flossie, there's a good girl.'

FLORENCE & SYDNEY PIKE
1908

Nevertheless it is bad taste; we make no attempt to deny it;
and it was, we think, a little cruel of the Greek Government
in 1924 to hold a state function at Sunium in commemoration
of Byron's having left the furrows of his clasp knife upon the
venerable temple. For a man who saw fit to have such a motto
as he had inherited – 'Crede Byron' – emblazoned on his
travelling bed, it can have been but a little thing. All the same,
it was unnecessary to emphasise it.

Nobody whom we had consulted in Athens had been able to recall the whereabouts of the name, and we had almost given up hope of finding it, when, while creeping along a narrow ledge by hugging each successive pillar, I suddenly noticed the five neat little italics within a few inches of my nose. In a fever of excitement we searched for the name of the best known of Byron's modern biographers who, rumour tells, has thought fit to add to the lustre of the poet's name by placing his own in close proximity to it. Our search proved in vain. Instead, immediately below the *BYRON*, appeared in meticulously careful print the youthful indiscretion of a man who is at present the principal of a famous Oxford College. As he can have but a few more years to live, we have decided to refrain from publishing his name.

Forsaking these uncouth relics, we descended by a long slope to a secluded bay, David and Michael to bathe, while I basked on a rock, nursing my cold. The others undressed on a sheltered spit of sand, and were swimming about, pink streaks in the limpid blue water of the tiny inlet; when suddenly from round behind a rocky promontory, in the same unexpected manner in which these things slide on to the stage at Covent Garden, glided the very quintessence of ancient Greece as visualised by modern painters – a boat, of almost mythical grace, tapering to a high curving prow and propelled by six long slender oars, the rowers of which were seated in two lines, three on one side and three on the other. It might have been the home-coming of Ulysses.

But the lovely barque had no sooner come to a standstill, than pandemonium was let loose upon the bathers' idyll. A swarm of barefooted fishermen, of all ages, with skins like crocodiles, grew from the rocks to meet their disembarking fellows. And the whole crowd of about twenty or thirty, divided into two groups, each of which seized on a hitherto invisible wire hawser, which they proceeded to haul in from the depths of the sea. They performed the most elaborate evolutions; one group was perched high up on the cliff, swaying as though to an inaudible hornpipe, while the other tugged and heaved below upon the sand. Then both lunged down twenty yards to the right and the wires swept me off my rock and threatened to lift David and Michael bodily out of the sea. Ten minutes' comparative regularity were followed by a re-formation to the left but down at the water's edge, so that the bathers were now irrevocably separated from their clothes. At length, far out upon the skyline, a row of floats could be seen hurrying in from Asia Minor. The efforts of the fishermen redoubled, and leaving David and Michael in peace, they formed up in two parallel lines upon the shore near me, and pulled for forty minutes. Gradually the floats, small, red barrels, drew near in two long diverging lines joining in a curve, like a magnet with its ends inwards. Here was a net a quarter of a mile in length, that must have swept a hundred acres of the sea. Slowly the barrels were hauled up. I craned eagerly forward; the men heaved; the net emerged in dense masses; not a winkle was to be seen. At last, with one superhuman wrench, the day's catch slithered over the side into the bottom of the boat. There were perhaps four bushel baskets of sprats, and one small grey octopus, which a man cleaned and laid upon the beach. As the tide immediately washed it away, we rescued it, but he exhibited no gratitude. This, then, was the living of twenty fishermen. David and Michael being now dressed, we clambered up the hill and into the car.

On the way home I felt that suicide would be a welcome relief from the irritation of my cold. But some *rezina*, the *vin ordinaire* of this country, which, being preserved with resin, tastes like the smell of a chemist's shop, succeeded in clearing my head. Its medicinal properties are not merely imaginary, and most English residents drink it for their health. We reached the Grande Bretagne in time for dinner, to find Simon very fresh, having just arisen. I took my bed that evening and stayed there the following day reading the Reminiscences of Lady Dorothy Nevill, which I had purchased in a bookshop round the corner. One sentence, written with all admiration in relation to the late

Lord Ellenborough, has remained in my mind as supremely typical of the Victorian female mentality:

'He used to say to me: "War and Women, these are in reality the only fit interests for a man!"'

It is a curious reflection on the late Victorian era – a reflection forcibly corroborated by the popular songs of the day – that the sole interests, if not occupations, of most of our grandparents, were immorality and slaughter.

CHAPTER IX

THERE IS ALWAYS a certain hour of the day in southern countries, when the sun being at its zenith, any margin of shade that is usually to be found, either on one side of the street or the other, disappears. The pedestrian drags himself through a glaring furnace, eyes half closed, clothes clinging, vitality at its lowest. It was during such a moment, one Wednesday morning, that two figures, a gentleman called Mr Coningsby, and myself, might have been seen traversing the lower end of Constitution Square, in the direction of the Rue Kolokotronis. After knocking at a front door approached by two steps, we were ushered up a narrow, twisted staircase into a lofty, double-windowed apartment, the walls of which were crowded with pictures, some of them seascapes, others portraits of prominent statesmen. On the floor stood a number of bookcases, tables and a desk; while in the middle of the room, resting on an easel as though in process of completion, was a large painting of fishermen beaching their boat against a stormy sunset. Perched on suitable ledges, hanging from nails, and piled in the mouths of electro-plate reproductions of ancient Greek vases, were to be seen sponges of every shade, texture, shape and size.

As we entered the doorway, there sprung toward us a broad, upright man of middle age, whose most noticeable features were a bristling, black moustache, heavy eyebrows, and a large head that was mostly bald. With a lightning movement, indicative of hidden vigour, he caught one of Coningsby's hands in both of his, and wrung it without ceasing, as the words of welcome came pouring from his mouth in harsh and stilted French.

This man, in whose rooms we now stood, was Dr Skevos Zervos, the exiled leader of the Dodecanesians, spongefisher, artist, OBE, representative of his native islands at Versailles, and Greek parliamentary deputy.

I was presented to him. He waved us to chairs. Coffee, fruit syrup, liqueurs and sticky, green, preserved oranges were brought in on trays and placed before us.

'But scanty hospitality!' cried the doctor. 'We islanders are a frugal, hard-living people. But such as it is, I beg you accept. My house is yours – everything I have!' And flinging out his arms he began to rummage among his papers, while Coningsby and I ate and drank.

'Leave nothing,' whispered Coningsby with superfluous caution.

Our conversation with Dr Zervos, which was conducted in French, lasted two hours. It resulted, a few months later, in an article entitled, 'The Dodecanese under the Italians', which appeared in the *New Statesman,* and was also transcribed on to the front page of the *Empros,* an Athenian daily newspaper, under the heading:

Η ΔΩΔΕΚΑΝΗΣΟΣ ΥΠΟ ΤΟΥΣ ΙΤΑΛΟΥΣ

This I felt to be the summit of literary fame – translation into the language of Homer. Meanwhile, additional information has come to hand. But before entering upon a detailed account of the present condition of the Dodecanese and the outstanding importance of these thirteen islands off the south west corner of Asia Minor in Mediterranean politics – facts of which the world at present appears to be entirely ignorant – it may not be irrelevant to attempt some short analysis of the most living political organism of our generation. The structure of Fascismo, its spirit and its trend, is the salient factor in the shifting policies of south eastern Europe.

As a work of internal reorganisation in a country unsuited by temperament to parliamentary government, the Fascist rule has proved an incontrovertible success. 'Our newspapers are suppressed, our famous men are murdered, our streets run blood – and then you tell us that our trains are more punctual' – such perhaps is the argument of Italian liberalism. But there is the other side. In matters of social welfare, education and industrial prosperity, Italy since 1922 has advanced as far as any country in the world. A population of 38,815,000 has since 1922 been increased by three millions. During the last quarter of 1925 more ships were constructed in Italian yards than in those of any country in the world with the exception of our own. And even though dance-halls are forbidden in Trieste and kissing in the streets of Florence, it must be generally admitted that Mussolini, the hounded socialist of former days, for whose re-entry into Switzerland to attend the Conference of Lausanne the Federal Government of that country was obliged to pass a special law – Mussolini, by his internal administration, has fully justified the rule of himself and the enthusiasm of his supporters.

Externally, the foreign policy of Fascismo is dictated by the exigencies of the domestic. Here lies its weakness. The bands of young men on which the whole political edifice rests, can only maintain their enthusiasm, their team spirit, their hold on the country, by the joint exercise of violence. The appetite is much the same as that which ordains compulsory football in English public schools. Unfortunately for Mussolini, internal opposition, either through terror or astute cunning, has dissolved. The Corfu incident, and subsequent pugnacious utterances, have so far kept his personality green in the eyes of his adherents. But the moment will arrive when the dictator must choose from two alternatives – his own downfall or the materialisation of his 'Napoleonic Year'. If, as has been said, he is already approaching the latter 'like an elephant on tiptoe', he has at least succeeded in creating such a clamour with the near fore-foot in the Tyrol, that Europe is now deafened to the direction of the other remaining three. It is not generally recognised that the Italian occupation and administration of the Dodecanese today present not only a complete negation of the accepted precepts of civilised government, but a definite menace to the peace of the Near East.

There is nothing new about Italian imperialism. Its innate vulgarity is as apparent in the Roman arches of triumph which still adorn the countries of the Mediterranean basin, as in the marble pillar-box which marks the Brenner frontier today. In the case of the Dodecanese its first manifestations were felt in the year 38 BC when Cassius, seizing Rhodes, 'inhumanly butchered the native ruling class, savagely plundering the city and carrying off more than three thousand statues... Such of the inhabitants as survived, together with the remnant population of the other islands, dragged on a miserable and oppressed existence under the Roman heel.'

The subsequent history of the islands has not been an enviable one. After a period of comparative independence as a province of the Byzantine Empire, they eventually fell a prey to the land-hunger of the ubiquitous Norman Crusader, and were consigned, in 1310, to the rule of the Knights of St John of Jerusalem, who, during the two centuries of their dominion, 'left behind them no single mark of civilising activity'. In 1532, after half a century of almost incessant fighting, they were forced to admit the suzerainty of the Turk; and Rhodes, once the cultural centre of the civilised world, the cradle of painting and sculpture and the sciences, of medicine and navigation – Rhodes, the most splendid of cities, where, according to Homer, Zeus had poured a ram of gold, where once had dwelt half a million citizens, was left stripped of her treasures, with a population of no more than 35,000 souls. For 380 years the infidel remained in occupation. At length, during the Tripoli war of 1912 (between Turkey and Italy) the Italian Admiral d'Aste Stella sailed across the Aegean and, with the aid of the inhabitants themselves, restored the Dodecanese once more to Christian governance.

The new political status, however, proved of a different quality to that which had been expected. 'At the end of the war (the Tripoli war) your islands shall receive an autonomous regime. I tell you this in my capacity as a soldier and a Christian, and I pray that you will regard my words as the words of the gospel.' So spake the Italian General Ameglio in a proclamation to the Rhodians in 1912. Unfortunately the Tripoli war was succeeded by the Balkan war; and the Italians had not completed their preparations for the evacuation of the islands, when the outbreak of hostilities in 1914 rendered their retention strategically unavoidable. However, in 1920, by the 122nd article of the Treaty of Sevres, signed and ratified by Italy, it was agreed that the words of the gospel should at length materialise, the twelve smaller islands being ceded to their mother country Greece; while in the event of the British renunciation of Cyprus, the fate of Rhodes was to be determined by plebiscite in 1935. This treaty, though never revoked, was superseded by that of Lausanne. But Lord Curzon, alive to the complications of the question, linked its final settlement with that of Jubaland. The diplomatic subtleties of this arrangement were rudely upset by the Labour Government of 1924, who, finding that an unprofitable African province was costing the treasury some £40,000 a year in maintenance, made a present of it to Italy without more ado. Meanwhile Greek Nationalism had been discredited by the disaster of Smyrna. The British, who had sent the Greeks to Asia Minor, primarily to prevent the Italians going there instead, made no attempt to preserve the Balance of Power in the Near East that they had created. And Italy, no longer hampered by the British and Greek occupations of Jubaland and Asia Minor respectively, has remained in the Dodecanese to this day, with a free hand to pursue her policy of Mediterranean imperialism.

Despite the usually questionable qualities of Turkish liberalism, it cannot be denied that until 1912, the islanders enjoyed a certain measure of independence. The following extract is taken from an edict issued by Mahommed II in 1835, on the occasion of the restoration of the ancient rights of Calymnos, Ikaria, Patmos and, Leros, forfeited during the

Greek war of Independence. 'At the same time' – that is to say simultaneously with the payment of the annual tribute – 'their affairs shall be conducted and completed according to their own wishes, by men whom they themselves shall elect every year.' Such autonomy presents a strong contrast to the process of Italisnisation at present in progress.

Practically all interinsular communication has been prohibited, the essential sense of interinsular unity being thus dissolved. Schools have been closed; while the masters of those that remain are compelled by law to go to Rhodes and learn Italian. Similarly, at the harbour towns, *all* street-signs and café notices must display, and all boatmen speak the alien language – for the benefit of tourists. This device has lately bamboozled several correspondents of the English press, and other usually accurate writers, who have been taken on personally conducted tours by the Italian officials of the Dodecanese. The alternative to Italian citizenship is exile; and this indeed is usually the fate of any educated Greek. The refugees arrive in Athens weekly. The Greek flag is taboo, and the inhabitants are painting their houses blue and white instead. To any Italian marrying a Dodecanesian who brings a dowry of land on which he can settle and appear indigenous, the Italian Government offers a reward of 5,000 lire – with one eye perhaps on the promised plebiscite. Religious processions, sanctioned for centuries by the infidel, are forbidden by the spiritual subjects of the Pope.

Materially the prosperity of the islands is rapidly on the decline. In 1912 they possessed 143,080 inhabitants; in 1917, 100,148. The figure has now sunk to less than 80,000. One example will suffice. The inhabitants of Calymnos have always been completely dependent for their living on the industry of sponge-fishing. This the Italians have deliberately prohibited in favour of their sponge-beds off the coast of North Africa. In 1912 the population of the island was 20,855; in 1917, 14,445. It is now barely 10,000.

While bearing in mind that Italy's entry into the war in 1915 was made conditionally on her retention of the islands, it may also be remembered that our new ally did all in his power to prevent the mobilisation of the Dodecanesians on behalf of the Entente. The following quotation from the *Nation* of January 25th, 1919, will illustrate the treatment accorded a people who were as anxious as the allies themselves to combat the joint forces of Ottoman and the Hun. 'The islanders are driven from their homes and there are already 60,000 refugees at the Piraeus. The remnant is threatened with starvation, and hundreds have already died of hunger. Yet these men fought bravely in the War, volunteering for service and going out in boats with land bombs to chase the German submarines. Why are they to be Italianised against every principle of Mr Wilson's peace?'

Meanwhile the Armistice was followed by spontaneous plebiscites in Rhodes and elsewhere, demanding reunion with Greece. The crowds were fired on by the *carabinieri,* and two women and a priest were killed. Late in 1925 some·schoolboys of Calymnos were beaten by the Italian soldiery for writing 'Long live Greece' on the walls of their town. There was a time when the powers protested at such happenings, when the beating of Polish children by the Prussians, or the massacre of St Petersburg in 1905, roused the Anglo-Saxon peoples to fury.

Today we are more apathetic. But though moral issues can make but little appeal to a public sensibility that has seen a whole generation of its manhood exterminated, there exists perhaps in the naval base at Leros, a more concrete ground for interest. Not only from the words of Dr Zervos, but from accounts of actual eye-witnesses, did Coningsby and I afterwards corroborate the facts of the transformation of this rocky islet, with its excellent harbour, into a fortified stronghold calculated to command both the west coast of Asia Minor and the route between two of the most important channels of international communication, the Suez Canal and the Bosphorus. Aeroplane hangars have been built and big naval guns installed; a submarine base has been constructed; and storehouses and barracks are in process of erection – a final proof, if one is needed, that the Italians regard their occupation of the islands as permanent. But what purpose can a military, as well as a naval and air base serve in such a position? The answer is to be found in the immense mineral wealth of Lycia, the south west province of Asia Minor, and the coalfields of Heraklea on the Black Sea. Both of these the Italians make no secret of their ambition to possess. And, as a collateral expression of the new Mediterranean imperialism, may be taken the arrival not long ago in the harbour of Valetta of two boat-loads of black-shirted Fascisti shouting 'Malta for the Italians'. In fact, to all intents and purposes, the followers of Mussolini appear, in the eyes of those few who are in a position to speak – independent visitors are not encouraged in the Dodecanese – to be preparing for a Mediterranean 'Der Tag', as surely as the Prussians were calculating the final subjection of France before 1914. Thus it is not surprising that the travesty of the Anglo-Italian debt settlement, synchronising as it did with our own dispute with the Porte over Irak, should have been regarded in certain quarters as cloaking some secret agreement of an anti-Turkish nature. That motive does actually lie behind the *rapprochement* that has momentarily sprung into being between Italy and Greece. Meanwhile the Dodecanesians suffer.

'How long will the present state of things continue?' I asked Dr Zervos.

'We hope for the assistance of England or the League of Nations,' he replied, 'or else...' He paused; then invoked the analogy of Crete, an island which, it will be remembered, carved its own independence.

'And now,' he continued, 'allow me to present you with the book I have written on the subject of the Dodecanese. I will send it round to you, if you will be so good as to write your name and address on a piece of paper.'

He handed me a pencil. As I wrote, his face seemed to light up; his eyes opened. Seizing both my hands in his, he swayed up and down in front of the long windows looking out on the hot sunlight of the narrow Athenian street, crying 'The new Byron! The new Liberator!'

England is not conscious of the veneration in which she is held by the country that she sponsored a century ago into a second being. The Byron legend is a living force; and it is to the English that the Dodecanesian Greeks look for their eventual deliverance from a regime that is robbing them not only of nationality, but their very means of livelihood. At the present time the man in the street is barely conscious even that the Dodecanese exists. But those individuals who are, cannot help feeling that it may not be long before the attention of the world is directed thither with unexpected suddenness. Of the death of Byron at 'Missolonghi, April 19th, 1824' John Drinkwater has written:–

Let Italy remember that the clarion cause may one day sound again.

CHAPTER X

IT WAS A BANK HOLIDAY. On such occasions the population of Athens eats garlic. Impelled by the unflagging energy of Howe, we decided, as many other bank holiday-makers have decided before, upon a day in the country. Our party consisted of David, Simon and myself, Howe and Michael, and Komara and Cartaliss. The chauffeur had formerly been in the employ of the Royal Family; and his car which, we were obliged to hire owing to Diana's indisposition, was built of wood on the lines of a summerhouse calculated to withstand bad weather. The heat was intense; burning dust and burning air scorched the exposed hands and face; while every portion of the body received the most acute blows as we lurched in and out of the dust-concealed craters, of which Greek roads consist. Once we stopped to pick grapes with which to quench our thirst; but as these themselves were almost boiling, it seemed better to wait until we could unpack the lunch that we had brought with us.

After about twenty miles, we forsook the main road for a small track, eventually coming to a stop beneath a group of large and shady olive trees. Beneath these were seated parties of men and women eating and drinking at long tables, some already hilarious; to the back were one or two low white houses and a little church; in front, the sea. Moored to the shore was a single boat, of the same classical proportions as that which we had seen at Sunium. Howe, bent beneath an enormous amphora of Cretan wine two feet in height and one in diameter, led the way on board, followed by the rest of the party, bearing sandwiches, figs, goats' cheese, grapes, eggs,

local beer, and one glass, which the boatman immediately sat
upon. We unloosed and sailed into the bay.

Porto Raphti had been, in medieval times, the main harbour
to Athens. The inlet, about two miles in width, is, like the
entire coast of Greece surrounded by hills rising sheer from
the sea, which curve right round to form a horseshoe. At the
opening of this stands a tiny but very high conical island the
approach to which is complicated by the presence of a small
flat-topped rock, tenanted by rabbits and green bushes, which
lies in front of it. Very leisurely we sailed over the surface of
the bay, tacking from side to side. David was given the tiller to
hold; and being unfamiliar with the evolutions of a sailing boat
sent us some distance out of our course.

Meanwhile we bathed. The water was alive. It seemed to
breathe. It was as though a million sun-warmed beryls and ice-
cold aquamarines were rushing silently over the skin; while a
fundament of sapphire was sucking at the feet. The whole body
shivered with conflicting exhilarations. Then as we lay about,
blinking at the sun and peering into the darkened clarity of the
depths, a soft gust of wind would drive the boat ahead; and
we would swim after it and clamber in, to sit and bake and eat
the goats' cheese and eggs, and drink the Cretan wine. Round
and round the enormous jar circulated, like some primitive
loving-cup; while the contents, a strong and burning, thick,
red drink, showed no signs of lessening. The boatman had his
own supply in a smaller pot.

Thus the afternoon passed. Had a strange tourist come upon
the scene, he would have been astonished to behold this cargo
of Ettys, Tukes and Alma Tademas, gliding like an oleograph
over the bosom of the ocean. Gradually the sun began to drop
in the heavens. And gradually we became aware that we were
making no progress. At length Komara took the tiller.

As we now drew closer, it became apparent that the island
fell sheer into the sea, save at one point, to reach which entailed
sailing between the rabbits on their rock and the further
uninviting shore. Though this channel, now that we approached

it, was a full three hundred yards in width, some combination of wind and current effectually prevented our accomplishing our objective. We tacked, we ran before the wind; we hauled up auxiliary sails at one end of the boat and let down others at the other. The wine upset; our clothes fell into the sea. We jumped from left to right and right to left, as the masts dipped into the waves and the main sail bellied in the air. Meanwhile the faintest syllable of breeze had vanished. Eventually, bereft of all hope, Simon and I threw ourselves miserably into the water, determined to make the island by some means or other. What had appeared to be a distance of about fifty yards, now expanded into a quarter of a mile. Gallantly we struggled on our voyage of exploration. As we neared the island, pebbles developed into boulders and boulders into cliffs. Faint with apprehension, we attained the first rocks. Above us the island rose like a gigantic spire. Below, fastened evilly upon their submarine promontories, the barbarous black points of myriad sea urchins threatened to harpoon our legs. With extreme care, we clambered from the water, and set off for the summit.

Meanwhile the others, guided by us, had succeeded in mooring the boat, and were following in our wake. Being shod they had the advantage of us. All nature had combined to hinder the ascent. Great, jagged cubiforms of rock, each facet sharpened to a razor-edge, alternated with every variety of thorned vegetation ever classified: creeping thorns and upright thorns; thorned ivy and thorned helibore; bushes displaying a regular octagonal mesh of thorns like rabbit-wire; thorns that protruded and shot back again like lizards' tongues. And in addition, insects: vast horseflies, clouds of invisible gnats; midges; bluebottles; hornets, wasps and bees. While large rats, that can have subsisted only on each other, slunk lethargically to cover as we passed. The crannies were filled with potsherds and old bones. Part of an unornamented vase we discovered and several fragments, cast in wavy lines. Also a flower, not unlike a columbine in shape, with white, fleshy petals and a purple middle, that smelt of all the honeys in the world and yet resembled none of them. At last, after half an hour's hard climbing, we topped the pin-point of the cone. And there, with her back toward us, seated majestically upon a pedestal of un-mortared blocks, was the statue, white against the sky, with the purple shadows of evening already darkening the white folds of her drapery. We had viewed her from the mainland, a dot upon her pinnacle. Close at hand she would have measured perhaps ten feet in height; and her plinth as high again.

Niccolo de Martoni, an Italian lawyer of the fifteenth century, made mention of yet another statue at Porto Raphti. A woman, the medieval legend ran, being pursued by a man, prayed that rather than fall into his clutches, both might be turned into stone. No statue, however, could ever have sat companion to that which now confronted us, placed as it was upon the very topmost point of a perfect cone. The older story is more beautiful, and at least as authentic. A wife, whose husband had sailed to the wars took up her residence upon the island, where she sat, day by day, surveying the horizon of the sea in expectation of his return. He never came. Summer and winter she watched. At last she died. And then, too late, he reappeared, and hearing the tale of her devotion erected this statue to her memory.

Thus she has sat for a quarter of a hundred centuries watching, ever watching. Gradually her hands, feet and even head, have been sacrificed to the greed of thieves and antiquarians. Yet wind and rain and sun have healed the wounds, worn smooth the scars. And for all their headlessness, the eyes still strain for the longed-for sail; the absent hands still rest impassively on the slightly parted knees. The day was drawing to its close. An amethyst light crept over the water. Far below, the islets and lower hills assumed a dark and cold blue tinge, as their eastern slopes fell into the twilight. Simultaneously, the purple and brown of their opposite faces caught the fire-opal lights of the setting sun. Long shadows moved over the sea. The sky deepened. A breeze blew out of the night and was gone. And the changeless marble figure, poised between earth and sky and sea, seemed to incarnate that land, a land oblivious of the conqueror, whether Frank, Venetian or Turk, the land of Homer and of Byron, of Pericles and Venizelos, for whom men of all epochs and nationalities have fought and died; for no other reason than that she is Greece.

During the descent John Lennox Howe performed one of those heroic acts of charity that enshrine men for ever in the hearts of their fellows. The feet of Simon and myself had become so cut and bruised that half-way down we found ourselves, even with the aid of dead mullein stumps, literally unable to move. For it was impossible to let the weight of the body fall upon the arms, as during the ascent. We were on the verge of tears from sheer pain, when the head of Howe, who had gone on ahead, suddenly reappeared beneath our feet. He had run down the whole way to the boat and returned with our shoes. By the time we were all embarked it was practically dark.

The wind had died down, and the boatman grew agitated as the lights began to twinkle out from the furthest distant inland point of the bay. Despite his entreaties, we insisted on another bathe; then took the oars and rowed in turns, with only the light to guide our direction. It was nearly eight o'clock by the time that the boat was moored to the miniature stone jetty where we had found it. A drone of singing came faintly from under the olive trees; and a group of human beings straggled out of the darkness to watch our arrival, as we hurriedly donned such of our clothes as could be found in the confusion. Still carrying the Cretan wine, we stepped gingerly ashore and felt our way along a little path lapped by the ripples, finally seating ourselves at a trestle table beneath one of the trees.

Around us were other long tables; and at them other parties of holiday-makers, now perhaps feeling the effects of the day's drinking; women in cotton dresses; men, swarthy and burned, with black moustaches and black felt hats. From the lower branches of the trees depended receptacles like milk-cans, on either side of which protruded little pipes. These gave forth flares of lighted acetylene, which cast bright gleams of light and long deep shadows as they swayed gently in the soft breeze. The door of the church was open and the amber light of invisible candles glowed faintly out of the darkness. At the back another lighted doorway betokened the inn. After calling for some beer, Komera rose and went inside. We were all tired after such a day in the water, and sat with our heads on our hands, half asleep. The Greeks chattered gently, or hummed a tune in floating, quavering voices, that seemed like the pipes of Pan borne down the ages. And through all, the sea murmured faintly against the earthen shore. Suddenly at one of the tables, the merriest, there was a combined straightening of shoulders and an in-taking of breaths; silence; a man's finger raised; then dropped; and there burst upon the listeners, like reed music over a valley, the delicate lilt of mashers and dundrearies: 'Ta ra ra ra boom de ray; Ta ra ra ra *boom* de ray; Ta *ra* ra ra boom de ray; Ta ra ra ra *boom*...'

Our trance was disturbed by the reappearance of Komara, bearing a dish of scrambled eggs and chopped bacon, cooked with his own hands. What other dish could have added such superlative ecstasy to a night already perfect? Eventually, scarcely able to keep awake, we sought the refuge of the car, whence we gazed at the stars and the acetylene flares silhouetting the olives and the shadowy revellers beneath them. At last we drove off back to Athens. The voices seemed to wail farewell, the sea to murmur softly, 'Come again'. Writing now, three months later, with the wind in the branches of the forest and a paraffin lamp illumining the snowflakes as they fall outside the window pane, it murmurs still, 'Come again. Come back. Come again. Come back. Come.'

CHAPTER XI

THE LAST SATURDAY IN SEPTEMBER was imminent; and with it, the last boat. The prospect of four nights in the Orient Express, was, for reasons of temperature and expense, not sufficiently attractive to warrant a few days' extra delay. I decided to leave midday on Saturday. The morning arrived. Simon said that he was coming too. I walked across Constitution Square and reserved two berths at Ghiolmamn's travel bureau. On my returning to pack, Simon decided not to come and went to his bath instead. Eventually the moment of departure materialised.

First appeared Michael's servant. For him we hired a car, in which, accompanied by my trunk, valise, and the deck chair that we had bought at Brindisi, he set off to Piraeus. Escorted by Michael, I went round and said goodbye to Howe in his office behind the Legation; and also to Atchley, who for thirty years has been the mainspring of Anglo-Greek relationships. In the midst of these farewells the Charge d'Affaires, named Rathbone, suddenly entered the room bearing a bronze cat that he had purchased at a booth in Shoe Lane – would I, if passing through Paris, convey it to an Armenian dealer in the Rue de la Paix, so that he, Rathbone, might learn whether it was genuine before paying for it? Naturally delighted to render any service to our diplomatic body, I wedged the animal into my overcoat pocket; and Michael and I, now joined by David, proceeded to the underground. The train was filled to bursting with the lunch-hour rush. When we reached Piraeus, the luggage had not yet arrived. We waited disconsolately about, then struggled through the customs and into a little boat – myself, Michael, Michael's servant, the overcoat, the luggage and the two boatmen. David, having no diplomatic pass, was forced to remain behind the railings with which the quay was surrounded. It was with feelings of despair that I bade him goodbye.

The boat pushed her way among her fellows like an angry bee in an angrier hive. Forty yards out, the *Andros,* of the Byron line, a drab and insignificant vessel, was pointed out as my homeward barque. The contemplation of four days and nights in her confined bosom left me stunned. We climbed up the side. Michael introduced me to a junior officer named Joannides. His French was scarcely better than mine, so that for the rest of the voyage we avoided one another like rival plagues. Then Michael said goodbye and went. The utter desolation of finding myself prisoner on a very small boat, in company with a cargo of strange Greeks, seemed almost insupportable. Tears welled to my eyes, as slowly we steamed out of harbour, and beyond the masts and funnels appeared the brown hills; the far-distant white-pillared Parthenon; Lykabettus; Hymettus and the mountains. I went below and stifled my grief in a plate of cold ham.

My cabin was next the dining room. It contained berths for four arranged in the form of two Ls. I appropriated the one immediately beneath the porthole, so that my dormitory-mate, whose name appeared from the passenger list to be Kalomati, should have no chance of regulating the supply of air. Suspecting, as was the case, that this berth had been allotted to him, I hastily unpacked my bag all over it. No sooner was this accomplished than there entered a small, stocky man with a bristling grey moustache, a ponderous, grizzled head, black tie, pearl pin, double-breasted coat, white flannels and parti-coloured shoes

'*Ah,*' he said, in a pleasant voice, '*Nous partagerons cette cabine.*'

'*Oui, M'sieur,*' I answered.

'Oh – you are English? You desire that berth? Very well. I too live in London. I have lived there for years.' It is curious how nearly all foreigners have.

He then unpacked his hair-brushes, a bottle of Bond Street hair lotion, a tweed cap with cast-iron creases in it, and a large assortment of coats and ties, obviously purchased at discreet establishments in Hanover Square and Jermyn Street. He immediately changed his clothes, a process which he repeated at intervals of two hours during the entire voyage. His time on deck was occupied in playing turkey-cock to the one or two doubtfully good-looking ladies on board. When they retired to be sick, he paced up and down like a gobbler in an empty hen-run. His manner towards myself came to resemble more and more that of a man doing his duty by his butler's son. He asked continuously whether I was not feeling sick, evidently hoping that I was, so that he might display his advantage over me. But he appreciated the open window; and he washed extensively; so that I forgave him everything:

The meals were excellent, and with free wine, were included in the fare. On the first evening I had the good fortune to seat myself next the only Englishman on board, a Mr Galbraith. He had a wife, came from Co. Carlow, lived in Lincolnshire, spoke with a Manchester accent and had travelled extensively 'representing his firm', in almost every country in the world. He would, in fact, have been in India now, but for the 'kiddies'. He wore a thin cloth suit of neat Glen Urquhart checks and a Homberg hat that was too small for him; though when casually loafing about deck, he appeared in a blazer of soft, blue material. Though his business in life was to put through contracts in all parts of the globe, he spoke not a word of any language but his own, with the exception of a few self-conscious syllables of restaurant Italian. We discussed Ireland. I made him talk of his travels. He knew South America intimately and said that I ought to go on one of the big liners to Buenos Aires – within two days' time a Sports' Committee and an Entertainments' Committee had been formed on board – and everything was organised. It was different from the *Andros*.

There were two families of Levantine Americans on board, fat flabby couples, one of which maltreated its children.

The other appropriated my deckchair and pinned its card thereto. This I threw into the sea, and in its place pencilled initials of my own. The remainder of the first-class passengers seemed composed of honeymooning couples, the men of which omitted to shave and wore pince-nez, while the women emerged every day in new and ill-fitting 'creations'. It was pretty to watch their gambols as they slapped one another's thighs at table and greedily eyed each successive dish as it moved gradually towards them.

The incidents of the voyage were few. I read a book by Baroness Von Hütten named 'Candy'; and another by Robert Hugh Benson, called 'An Average Man', which I found on board and eventually stole in exchange for several others. This work describes with almost painful accuracy the hold which the Roman Catholic Church can obtain upon people suffering from a drab and riftless round of life; and how the sudden access of material interests can dispel this curious influence, as inexplicable as that of women. For the rest of the time I gazed at the horizon.

We passed the Straits of Messina at dawn, and the Straits of Bonifacio in the evening. Stromboli, which lies a little North of Sicily, presented an appearance of exquisite symmetry: a huge flat-topped cone rising the colour of bloom on ancient chocolate, from the deep blue of the Italian sea. Giant furrows, caused by the lava, showed in dark relief in the brilliant sunlight. At the foot of the island, infinitely small, clung the specks of a little white village. And above floated the curves and wreaths of fat, white, downy smoke, shading gradually away like strands of unspun silk into the blue.

The morning of the fifth day dawned to find us battling against rain, wind and a choppy sea, along the forbidding crag-strewn coast of Southern France. By degrees the twin spires of the Church of Notre-Dame de la Garde took shape, faintly black in the greyness, dominating from their eminence the whole, vast town of Marseilles. It was an hour or more before we had negotiated the various moles of the harbour.

Galbraith and I waited until the ship was almost empty, took one last look at her wild boar mascot, and stepped ashore into an enormous warehouse, where we placed our luggage in the hands of a Cook's man. Galbraith, being unable to utter more than the word '*combien*', and that with no great certainty, insisted on my bargaining with each cabman in turn; so that some time elapsed before we reached the Hotel Splendide. We then went shopping, as he wished to buy some scent for his wife. Having done so, we drank vermouth. It seemed odd to be sitting at a café now beneath a grey sky, with spits of rain falling on the pavement, and a cold autumn breeze beginning to shake the leaves from the plane trees. After lunching to the strains of a pretentious though melancholy band, we went to see a film, depicting Laura la Plante in a fast motor-boat drama. Five o'clock found us at the station and the Cook's man giving us our tickets and helping us into our carriage.

We had an early dinner. At Avignon a Frenchman and his wife joined us and proceeded to sleep in the other two corners. I got out at every opportunity to take the air.

We reached Paris about half past seven next morning and Galbraith hurried off to catch the half past eight train, as he was going to a theatre that night with his wife. I went to an hotel and had some breakfast, then delivered the cat and its message to the Armenian dealer, and walked down the Rue de Rivoli. In a window I saw Oliver Baldwin's new book, 'Six Prisons and Two Revolutions', and bought it. Catching the 12.30 at the Gare du Nord, I read it with interest – another testimony to the Betrayal Era in English statesmanship.

The channel steamer took less than an hour to cross. On board, as always, was one of those people with whom it is never quite certain whether one is on speaking terms or not. He was bringing over to England a patent device for transforming bottles of sparkling wine into syphons, once they had been opened. He had been spending a month in Paris and said that as far as he could see the French cocotte was beginning to find a dangerous rival in the American girl-tourist.

'Even in Paris?' I answered.

'Good gracious, yes! Why, the other night, for instance, James and I were sitting in the lounge, when...'

At Dover, our heavy luggage being registered, we had no trouble with the customs. We reached Victoria about seven. At eleven o'clock my trunk arrived, and I took it to the Paddington Hotel, which was full. After enquiries at several others, the Great Central Hotel at Marylebone offered me a camp-bed in a bathroom. I was thankful to accept it. My train reached home early next day, and it was with a feeling of supreme content that I motored down the avenues of the forest, with the morning sun falling through the beeches on to bracken already beginning to turn yellow.

Two months later I met David and Cartaliss over a cocktail. They had had a cold and adventurous journey home and had been delayed for a week in Belgrade. Finally they had broken down at Folkestone. Simon had plunged immediately into his obscure groove of life east of Piccadilly Circus. Cartaliss was off to Paris. I seized a minute on a foggy afternoon to walk with him round Oxford. The lights were beginning to come out. The decaying stone of the colleges, with tired figures wandering to their after-football baths, loomed sadly through the mist. Cartaliss said that he had never imagined that any place could be so Gothic. Then we drove out in the dark to a small raftered inn on the Upper Thames and had a drink of beer by the light of an open fire. From outside could be heard faintly the everlasting rumble of the weir. I had stayed here once in early childhood. The sheets on the bed had not been clean and my mother had had them changed. The world seemed larger now than it had done then in 1909. Private school, public school, university, intermittent trips abroad, intermittent Wiltshire; and last of all this tour had all intervened. Leaning forward to warm my hands over the logs, I experienced a new pride of race: the pride of being, as well as English, European.

BIOGRAPHICAL NOTE

Robert Byron was born in Wembley in 1905. He was educated at Eton and Merton College, Oxford, from which he was sent down with a third class degree for his persistently unruly behaviour. In 1925 he embarked with two friends on a car journey to Athens, a trip he would detail in his first book *Europe in the Looking Glass* (1926). In 1929 Byron became a correspondent for *The Daily Express*, and in 1933 published *First Russia, Then Tibet* based on his experiences of travel those countries.

It was also in 1933 that Byron set off on a ten-month trip across the Middle East and South Asia with his close friend Christopher Sykes. The resultant book *The Road to Oxiana* (1937) is considered to be not only Byron's finest, but one of the pre-eminent works of travel-writing in the English language. It was to be Byron's last major work. By the time he returned to Britain in 1936 the clouds of war were already gathering. He attended the 1938 Nuremberg Rally with Unity Mitford out of interest, but was no admirer of Nazism, which he described as 'intellectual and spiritual death'.

In February 1941 Byron was on board the SS *Jonathan Holt* when it was torpedoed in the North Atlantic en route to Cairo. Although officially a special correspondent for the BBC's Overseas News Department, rumours persist that he was involved in espionage on behalf of the Allied war effort. Byron was among fifty-two passengers and crew members lost; his body was never recovered.

Jan Morris was born in Somerset in 1926, living and writing under the name James Morris until undergoing sex reassignment surgery in 1972. Morris was educated at Lancing College and Christ Church College, Oxford. Having served in the Second World War, Morris became a foreign correspondent and was the first journalist to report the success of the 1953 British expedition to climb Mount Everest. She has published over forty books on a variety of subjects, and now lives in Wales.

SELECTED TITLES FROM HESPERUS PRESS

Author	Title	Foreword writer
Pietro Aretino	*The School of Whoredom*	Paul Bailey
Pietro Aretino	*The Secret Life of Nuns*	
Jane Austen	*Lesley Castle*	Zoë Heller
Jane Austen	*Love and Friendship*	Fay Weldon
Honoré de Balzac	*Colonel Chabert*	A.N.Wilson
Charles Baudelaire	*On Wine and Hashish*	Margaret Drabble
Giovanni Boccaccio	*Life of Dante*	A.N.Wilson
Charlotte Brontë	*The Spell*	
Emily Brontë	*Poems of Solitude*	Helen Dunmore
Mikhail Bulgakov	*Fatal Eggs*	Doris Lessing
Mikhail Bulgakov	*The Heart of a Dog*	A.S. Byatt
Giacomo Casanova	*The Duel*	Tim Parks
Miguel de Cervantes	*The Dialogue of the Dogs*	Ben Okri
Geoffrey Chaucer	*The Parliament of Birds*	
Anton Chekhov	*The Story of a Nobody*	Louis de Bernières
Anton Chekhov	*Three Years*	William Fiennes
Wilkie Collins	*The Frozen Deep*	
Joseph Conrad	*Heart of Darkness*	A.N.Wilson
Joseph Conrad	*The Return*	Colm Tóibín
Gabriele D'Annunzio	*The Book of the Virgins*	Tim Parks
Dante Alighieri	*The Divine Comedy: Inferno*	
Dante Alighieri	*New Life*	Louis de Bernières
Daniel Defoe	*The King of Pirates*	Peter Ackroyd
Marquis de Sade	*Incest*	Janet Street-Porter
Charles Dickens	*The Haunted House*	PeterA ckroyd
Charles Dickens	*A House to Let*	
Fyodor Dostoevsky	*The Double*	Jeremy Dyson
Fyodor Dostoevsky	*Poor People*	Charlotte Hobson
Alexandre Dumas	*One Thousand and One Ghosts*	
George Eliot	*Amos Barton*	Matthew Sweet
Henry Fielding	*Jonathan Wild the Great*	Pete Ackroyd

F. Scott Fitzgerald	*The Popular Girl*	Helen Dunmore
Gustave Flaubert	*Memoirs of a Madman*	Germaine Greer
Ugo Foscolo	*Last Letters of Jacopo Ortis*	Valerio Massimo Manfredi
Elizabeth Gaskell	*Lois the Witch*	Jenny Uglow
Théophile Gautier	*The Jinx*	Gilbert Adair
André Gide	*Theseus*	
Johann Wolfgang von Goethe	*The Man of Fifty*	A.S. Byatt
NikolaiGogol	*The Squabble*	Patrick McCabe
E.T.A. Hoffmann	Mademoiselle de Scudéri	Gilbert Adair
Victor Hugo	*The Last Day of a Condemned Man*	Libby Purves
Joris-Karl Huysmans	*With the Flow*	Simon Callow
Henry James	*In the Cage*	Libby Purves
Franz Kafka	*Metamorphosis*	Martin Jarvis
Franz Kafka	*The Trial*	Zadie Smith
John Keats	*Fugitive Poems*	Andrew Motion
Heinrich von Kleist	*TheMarquise of O–*	Andrew Miller
Mikhail Lermontov	*A Hero of OurTime*	Doris Lessing
Nikolai Leskov	*Lady Macbeth of Mtsensk*	Gilbert Adair
Carlo Levi	*Words are Stones*	Anita Desai
Xavier deMaistre	*A Journey Around my Room*	Alain de Botton
André Malraux	*The Way of the Kings*	Rachel Seiffert
Katherine Mansfield	*Prelude*	William Boyd
Edgar Lee Masters	*Spoon River Anthology*	Shena Mackay
Guy de Maupassant	*Butterball*	Germaine Greer
Prosper Mérimée	*Carmen*	Philip Pullman
Sir Thomas More	*The History of King Richard III*	Sister Wendy Beckett
Sándor Petöfi	*John the Valiant*	George Szirtes
Francis Petrarch	*My Secret Book*	Germaine Greer
Luigi Pirandello	*Loveless Love*	
Edgar Allan Poe	*Eureka*	Sir Patrick Moore
Alexander Pope	*The Rape of the Lock and A Key to the Lock*	Peter Ackroyd

Antoine-François Prévost	*Manon Lescaut*	Germaine Greer
Marcel Proust	*Pleasures and Days*	A.N.Wilson
Alexander Pushkin	*Dubrovsky*	Patrick Neate
Alexander Pushkin	*Ruslan and Lyudmila*	Colm Tóibín
François Rabelais	*Pantagruel*	Paul Bailey
François Rabelais	*Gargantua*	Paul Bailey
Christina Rossetti	*Commonplace*	Andrew Motion
George Sand	*The Devil's Pool*	Victoria Glendinning
Jean-Paul Sartre	*The Wall*	Justin Cartwright
Friedrich von Schiller	*The Ghost-seer*	Martin Jarvis
Mary Shelley	*Transformation*	
Percy Bysshe Shelley	*Zastrozzi*	Germaine Greer
Stendhal	*Memoirs of an Egotist*	Doris Lessing
Robert Louis Stevenson	*Dr Jekyll and Mr Hyde*	Helen Dunmore
Theodor Storm	*The Lake of the Bees*	Alan Sillitoe
Leo Tolstoy	The Death of Ivan Ilych	
Leo Tolstoy	Hadji Murat	Colm Tóibín
IvanTurgenev	*Faust*	Simon Callow
Mark Twain	*The Diary of Adam and Eve*	John Updike
Mark Twain	*Tom Sawyer, Detective*	
Oscar Wilde	*The Portrait of Mr W.H.*	Peter Ackroyd
Virginia Woolf	*Carlyle's House and Other Sketches*	Doris Lessing
Virginia Woolf	*Monday or Tuesday*	Scarlett Thomas
Emile Zola	*For a Night of Love*	A.N.Wilson